Forest Friends

of the

Night

by

Keith Bearden

Forest Friends of the Night

COPYRIGHT PAGE

ISBN-13: 978-1506101651

FOREST FRIENDS OF THE NIGHT
COPYRIGHT 2015 KEITH BEARDEN
ALL RIGHTS RESERVED

PUBLISHED BY RS PUBLISHING & DISTRIBUTION
HTTP://WWW.GHOSTSOFRUBYRIDGE.COM/RS-PUBLISHING-AND-DISTRIBUTION/

PRINTED BY CREATE SPACE, INC.
WWW.CREATESPACE.COM

PRINTED IN USA

ISBN-13: 978-1490567846

EDITED BY: THOMAS D. "THOM" CANTRALL

COVER: COVER PHOTO COURTESY OF DAN NEDRELO

Table of Contents

Foreword

by
Thom Cantrall

In the course of an average year, I will hear thirty to forty people with the idea of doing a book chronicling their experiences in the world of sasquatch or bigfoot as he is known variously. Of these thirty to forty ideas, I find that ten or so actually have merit in the subject covered and the experience of the person relating the story. Of these ten workable ideas, three will see actual work done and maybe one will be completed. The completed works that are worthy of purchase have become exceedingly rare in the recent past with most being merely a compilation of various reports from people around the country or continent.

Here we have something totally different. In this work, Keith is describing his own journey of discovery of these enigmatic people. When he first came to me with the idea, I was reluctant because I knew of the statistics cited above. I also knew how the haters and trolls would react as well. There are those who seem to live simply for the opportunity to denigrate others who have experienced something they have not. Their vitriol knows no bounds and their tolerance for new concepts and ideas is non-existent. I did not wish this on Keith... he is good friend and I knew what was in store.

Further, I knew how hard it was to get a book project completed. It is difficult to begin, follow through and end a story in good order, without digressing beyond the permitted range and maintaining interest of the reader. After all, I have attempted it with five books of my own...

I was pleasantly surprised as I began the editing process for his efforts. His story was logical... if followed a consistent path from event to event in a journey of discovery that rivals that of anyone I know. His presentation of the facts of his discoveries are well documented and are substantiated. This is not one person's pipe dream of what was happening... it is a logical sequence of events leading to some major revelations in time and account.

It is my extreme pleasure to have been a minor part of

this project and, since I was present for major portions of it, I can lend my support to the veracity of what happened on those nights he describes so well concerning our gatherings in his home state of Georgia.

I am quite regularly excoriated for not providing "proof" to a doubting and doubtful public and I respond in a common and like manner to all such. "It is not my place to provide proof to anyone of anything. The most I can do is offer evidence and since there is such wonderful evidence already available, mine would merely be redundant. There is the magnificent 'Patterson-Gimlin Film'... there is Paul Freeman's film... there is the 'Memorial Day Footage'... there is the 'Provo Canyon Footage'... there is the testimony of EXPERTS in their field... Men like Bill Munns, John Chambers and Peter Brooke have all made definitive statements and offered proof of the veracity of the existence of sasquatch."

My advice at this point now becomes, "If you want further proof, it is up to you to take the steps to provide it to yourself..." If those men listed above are not sufficient for you, then only you can prove it to yourself. That's what I did... I proved it to my own satisfaction...

Today, I no longer argue the point with anyone... I share what I observe... I teach those who would learn... and I ignore the rest... This book is a wonderful teaching tool to all of those who would use it as such.

Thom Cantrall

Prologue

This book is the story of my journey into the surreal world of believers of a large bi-pedal being that is known by many names. Bigfoot, sasquatch, yeti, abominable snowman, wendigo, yowie and many other native people's names describe an enigma. What once was something I thought to be a myth has changed my life totally and completely. This has been a journey of wondrous proportions and I have progressed through this with lots of guidance from friends.

There are so many people that have helped me along this journey and I know I can't possibly thank everyone. Thanks to Arla Collett Williams, Thom Cantrall, Alex Midnight Walker, Ron Morehead, Scott Nelson, Autumn Williams and Melba Ketchum. I appreciate the many hours you all devoted to helping me understand and teaching me to embrace the phenomena instead of denying it. Learning has certainly helped me overcome the fear and has led to not only the understanding of these magnificent beings, but of myself. I am amazed by how so simple a thing as that we call respect has led to the unlocking my new way of looking at everything.

I also would like to thank my wife Cathy who has stood firmly with me through our years. Her support of me has made all of this possible. She has believed in me when I shared with her things that have happened and this has helped me move forward. I now get to share with her those moments of discovery and learning.

Quote; Joichi Ito

"In a world where discovery is more important than delivery, it's the people who find, remix and direct attention to old stuff that should be rewarded, not the people who deliver it or sit on it waiting for someone to show up."

Forest Friends of the Night

1. The "Monster" In My Mind

As a small kid growing up in a suburb of Atlanta, Georgia, I only passed through the city when I was traveling a local Interstate Highway. We never ventured there except for the time my parents took me to the zoo.

Seeing the animals there, I sometimes wondered if there were any wild type animals that lived in the woods behind my house. Of course, my young mind would create them... especially at night. I would hear noises and strange bird calls and automatically I would imagine a big hairy monster back there. Even though it was just a small patch of woods in my mind it was a big jungle full of animals of all kinds.

My parents lived on a limited, fixed income and our budget didn't allow for much in the way of extra activities but we liked such activities as camping. Occasionally we would go to the drive in theater and, because of limited funds, my parents would sneak me in under a blanket in the back seat. We would watch the double feature and if there was anything I was not supposed to see, my Mom would make me cover my head with the blanket. When I grew to be a few years older and my baby brother took my place, he got the honor being "blanket censored".

I was ten years old when the preview of coming attractions featured a movie titled, "The Legend of Boggy Creek". As I watched the previews, I remember being frightened to the point I was afraid to go outside when it was close to getting dark. We, too, had a creek running through the woods behind us and I knew without a doubt there was the same monster living back there.

To make matters worse, I saw news features that talked about a creature called bigfoot and I saw the Patterson-Gimlin film for the first time. I thought to myself, it was amazing looking but it didn't seem as scary as I had first thought. It looked more human than what I had imagined. As I grew older, I would sometimes see articles in magazines or papers talking about the commonly named bigfoot.

I was extremely fascinated by that creature along with such others as the Yeti, Abominable Snowman etc. However, I knew IF they existed they were far from where I lived and were only scattered through the Pacific Northwest and in the Himalayan Mountain ranges. The media version of the "Monster" was implanted firmly into my mind.

2. My Love for the Outdoors

My father instilled in me, at the very early age of five, the love for being outside and of fishing, camping and hunting. We raised beagles to hunt rabbits and, although I was a child, going out with him to "run the beagles" got me into the woods often. Although I didn't carry a shotgun, Dad did let me take my pellet rifle. I would be outside hoping I could help bring rabbits home for dinner.

Many times we met an old man old man I knew simply as Mr. Cook in an area just west of Atlanta next to the Chattahoochee River. We often let the dogs run until late evening until or even until it got dark. One particular night he mentioned a time that someone in the area claimed to see a bigfoot in the area and he began taking a pistol with him when he came here. Was the "monster" really in Georgia too? My curiosity had peaked regarding what they really were and IF they really were... I read everything I could find at the library. Every so often a news report would be on television and there was even an occasional documentary shown.

Although I was still curious about this creature, I found that, as a teenager, my love for hunting and the outdoors grew. More and more, I wanted to be outside fishing, hunting, hiking, and camping. If I was outside, I was happy and my fear of the "monster" eventually disappeared totally. Days of hunting now occupied my mind... and deer hunting was especially important and what I enjoyed most with Dad.

Helping provide the much loved venison was something I felt made me more mature and being able to help Dad supply meat for our freezer was very satisfying to me growing up. As I grew into an older teenager, I became very proficient at hunting as well as tracking. I loved the challenge of it all and this was a way of life for us. Dad

He always stressed to me, "NEVER shoot anything

unless it is to eat. " He told me many, many times, "You harvest animals for food. If you kill it, you will eat it." I learned and understood that the purpose was not to kill, but to harvest what God has provided. Eventually, the excitement of the hunt was surpassed by the sheer thrill of being out in the woods and watching them awaken in the morning. What a wonderful feeling it was to breathe fresh air, see the sunrise and enjoy being alive.

3. The Noises in the Night

On our hunting lease we camped often. It is near the small town of Talbotton in west central Georgia though several miles distant from the closest town. We were located approximately two miles from the main road. Our four hundred and fifty acres was surrounded by thousands of acres of land unapproachable without a very long hike in some extremely dense forests.

Occasionally, there would be new sounds that I could not identify. Often, we would hear sticks breaking around camp but assumed that deer could be the ones responsible. We would, at times, hear screams from the creek that sounded similar to a cow, initially, but would rise in pitch and intensity until it sounded like a woman screaming. We assumed these were bobcats or some other night creature but never would we think to attribute these sounds to a bigfoot or anything of that sort. Because our mind usually associates unknown sounds into a known source, we thought nothing of it. The sounds, however, continued to recur over the next ten years or so. We would then joke about the "Boogey Man" which was always something our Grandparents and others would talk about. We, of course, knew the "Boogey Man" wasn't real, but the joke stood.

One night after an evening hunt in which Dad had connected on a shot at a buck that could not be immediately recovered, my cousin and I were called on to track it and find it. With the aid of a lantern and flashlights, we walked through the dense woods looking for sign. On this task, we became extremely aware of something walking just a few feet away in the very thick brush. We would walk and it would walk... We would stop and it would stop. We thought it was possibly a coyote tracking a wounded deer with us. That was the only possibility in our minds. We would occasionally hear a stick break... some were obviously too big for a coyote to have broken. We kept on the trail until we found the deer... Our concerns over the noise made us both a little nervous but we stayed on task and got the deer out and went back to camp.

While sitting by the fire a few hours later, my cousin asked, "What do you think that was following us?"

I, of course, didn't know, but the only thing I could associate was a coyote. I replied, "It must have been a coyote."

These type noises became common for us. One night Dad and I were camping. We were awakened by something that shook our tent and I turned on the flashlight to see what had caused the disturbance. Maybe a limb had fallen? I woke up Dad and we unzipped the tent. We looked around and saw nothing. Dad stayed out for a minute to answer a call of nature and then came back into the tent. We zipped back in and after a few minutes began to drift back to sleep. It was then Dad told me something had just pushed the side of the tent in. He said it had actually touched the cot on which he was sleeping. He then said, "it must be a raccoon..." We settled in our minds as it being just that.

Over the next few years, we heard noises at night more and more often. There were bird sounds at night when those birds were supposed to be roosting. The barred owl sounds were heard every single night and sometimes almost all night long. We commented often on hearing them so close so often, but we would never see one. One night we heard a horse whinny right behind our camp and very close. It circled our camp for a few minutes until we eventually took flashlights and walked some of the All-Terrain Vehicle trails and wait for it to get close. As it neared the trails and dirt road, we would switch on the lights trying to see it... We never could as it would switch directions and go on another route when the lights came on. This continued for at least thirty minutes at a session until, eventually, it was gone. We never saw it so we chalked it up as another noise in the night.

4. High Strangeness

Being outdoors to me was always magical. I loved watching wild animals going through their daily routines. We had deer, turkeys, squirrels, coyotes and the many other animals and they were always wonderful to watch. Actually hunting for game animals became secondary to simply watching them for

me. Being in the woods so many days through the years enabled me to learn very much about living life there. To hear certain sounds like squirrels barking, deer grunting during the rutting season to find a mate or ward off a rival, certain bird calls and many others was beyond special. These were imprinted on my brain as being the normal sounds of the woods.

I could actually "tune myself in" to my surroundings. I could use my mind's eye to hear the crow or the jay calling an alert and I knew certain predators like bobcats or coyotes might be lurking close by. I often thought of my Native

Forest Friends of the Night

American ancestors and how much better they were at this than I was since they were outdoors virtually every day. Sometimes I would hear things I could not identify and that became more frequent over the ensuing year or two.

There is one day in particular that I especially recall. I had taken time off from work during the middle of the week to go to our hunting property. I was hunting deer and sitting in an area of dense undergrowth. As I sat there quietly, I heard a commotion in the nearby brush that startled me. I could see movement and then a doe came bounding out of the brush at full speed. This alerted me of the potential for being a buck near. This was common when the bucks were chasing does to mate and, at this time, the deer rut was in full swing.

Nothing ever came out of the brush and after a few minutes of hearing no other noises; I relaxed and dropped my gun down. I then became aware of a very strong and powerful odor coming from the thicket which the doe had bounded. I began to wonder if there was a dead animal over there and that, perhaps, the deer had walked up on it and it had startled her.

I heard, a loud "POP"... I had no idea what had caused that, but it came from that same area. I looked at the area very closely and saw something dark there... As I watched, it moved smoothly and quietly through the brush. I could barely see its movement as it made its way up a hill, and away from me. When it topped the hill, three loud and steady pops echoed through the little draw of hardwoods on the other side of the crest. Almost immediately that was followed by three more identical pops that came from behind me, which was the same direction from which came the doe that ran off. I then noticed the smell was completely gone and all was quiet.

As darkness began to envelop the area, I was still thinking about what that could have been. I could not logically figure out the strange event that had taken place over the thirty minutes prior.

I stood and headed back to camp. As I got close to my truck, I heard the loud, mournful cry of an alpha coyote followed by the rest of the pack barking and howling all at the same time. This went on for only about a minute before they stopped. There was total silence... It was almost like you had simply turned off a switch. I could not hear a thing... not a bird... not a cricket... not a frog...there was simply nothing! Feeling a bit uneasy and nervous, I hurried back to camp at that point. Once back at camp, I fumbled in the dark to get the lantern lit. Normally I would have built a fire and sat out by myself, but on this night, I ate quickly and went to bed!

The next morning, after a good sleep, I awoke to the sounds of other hunters who had arrived into camp after I was retired. I poured myself coffee and went out to meet my cousin Farrel and his son in law Adam. I didn't mention anything to them and we quickly readied ourselves to head out to hunt. We went to our areas and it was beautiful. It was sunny, clear and cold... perfect weather to be outdoors. That morning's hunt was typical... I saw a few does and a small buck.

As I headed back to camp, I detoured to the area where I had heard the sounds the evening before. I found some hardwood trees approximately five inches in diameter were snapped into two pieces. I looked carefully to see if there were rubs on the tree from a buck's antlers, thinking a deer might have done it as this a typical behavior during the rut. They do this as a sign to other bucks to stay out. As I looked closely, there were no sign on the tree that would have indicated it was a rub tree. These trees had no scratches on them and appeared to me to have been simply broken off and pushed over. Even more interesting was the fact that the breaks were about five feet high! We have no elk in Georgia, only whitetail deer. The normal rub was about two to four feet off the ground at a maximum. I was at a loss to name what could have done this and not left a scratch on the tree.

By the time I arrived back at camp, Farrel and Adam were out of the woods as well and were standing by their camper. I walked over to see what they had seen while hunting. Farrel said he had seen a few deer. He then told Adam, "Tell him what you heard".

Adam hesitated for a minute then said, "I heard an Ape or Gorilla."

I looked at him and asked him; "What?" thinking they were joking.

He said, "No, I heard what sounded exactly like what you would hear in a Tarzan movie." He continued, "It was really close to me and I heard it for like thirty minutes off and on. I finally stood up and came back to camp because it was making so much noise."

Forest Friends of the Night

There was another time when we found a stack of deer skulls and neck vertebrae next to our camp. They were small and appeared to be those of fawns.  Strangest of all was there were no other bones at all. Why were these in a stack and no other bones found? If they had died there, there should have been more bones. If coyotes had left them, they would not have stacked them and left just those bones. It was a very weird event.

 We also began finding huge tree limbs snapped off of hardwood trees. These snaps were anywhere from a few feet to fifteen feet off the ground. They seemed to appear almost daily and in new places!

Forest Friends of the Night

On another occasion, my cousin came back to camp and made the statement, "I had the weirdest thing happen while hunting. I heard something growl at me! Then, there was total silence! No birds, no crickets or anything. It was strange!"

My son and I, in order to figure out this high strangeness, went to walk along the creek that crossed the entire property. We felt that, if there was an animal like a bear or something, it would eventually come to water and leave prints. We walked slowly, looking for anything to give us a clue. One of the things we found odd, was that in several areas we would find scat on rocks on the middle of the creek. It was not cat, raccoon, possum or any other animal I was familiar with. This was human looking except larger in diameter. We found three or four of these piles along the mile long stretch.

When we arrived in the area where my cousin had been growled at, we walked along the edge of the creek and found a tree structure shaped like a tepee. There was a great quantity of deer hair there in the trail. It appeared the deer could have been trapped or caught there as there was a hand full of hair but no sign of blood at all.

My world changed here in a moment... There, in a sandbar was a very fresh track! It looked exactly like a human bare foot except it was much wider. I then remembered the bigfoot shows I had seen on television and listening to Dr. Jeff Meldrum talk about them. I was so astounded! I couldn't believe what I was looking at! It took some time for the truth of the matter to register with me. To this day, the sight of that track is brilliant in my mind's eye.

5. The Journal

I decided I needed to try and figure out what was going on. I had a fifteen year old son and if something was out here that could hurt him, I wanted to know. To his end, I decided to begin keeping a journal. I felt that simply typing a report of each visit there would allow me to use the information to find someone that could help me on this that know more about the situation.

A quick search on the internet led me to the Bigfoot Field Researcher's Organization. As I scrolled through the reports I found many very similar experiences to mine. As a result, I joined the group and began posting what I was seeing and hearing. It wasn't long and I was contacted by their representative with whom I could arrange a meeting. Following is a report from the journal I kept over the next several months.

The first report – Posted: December 14th, 2009 10:02 PM
I have hunted on the same property for over thirty years.

We have seen and heard some weird things in that time and I really think we may have a Sasquatch on our property.

Let me explain further. Last year, my brother saw something huge and black walking through the woods about a hundred yards away. I thought at that time, he must have seen a bear, although we have never seen or heard of a bear as far south of the north Georgia Mountains as we are... about thirty miles north of Columbus Georgia.

This year began with loud screams we heard on a multiple occasions. My fifteen year old son and my dad heard one, and my son and I heard the other. At that time, we thought maybe it was a cat although it really sounded deeper. I really had never heard anything like it. A few weeks later, a couple of our hunters were standing and talking with us. They were telling us of a "monkey" they had heard. I questioned them further and they both said it sounded like a big gorilla or chimpanzee. They were totally serious.

Dad and my son heard the same sound a couple of weeks later. When I returned home, I began searching for sounds and I ran across some that were pretty close to what my son described so I let him hear them. He said the sounds were almost identical to what he had heard. They were supposedly bigfoot sounds that I had found on a website. I had become interested and was determined to discover what these noises were. The more I researched, the more I thought it could very well possibly be a bigfoot.

I have searched our property for the tree limb markers that I have read about. As of this date, I have seen a tree broken off and limb twists about five and ten feet off of the ground. I have heard what I thought were wood knocks on a few occasions. There were more interesting things that happened.

My parents were camping with my son during the archery season and they were sleeping in their pick up with a camper shell prior to me pulling their camper down. As they were sleeping

something hit the side of the truck waking up my mother as well as their dog who was sleeping with them. The dog began barking loudly enough to wake my dad. My mom told him what had happened, causing him to look outside. Unfortunately, he didn't see anything... Not too surprising since he doesn't see well without his glasses.

Second report - Posted: December 17th, 2009 11:36 PM

I spoke to a Bigfoot Field Research Organization (BFRO) investigator this week and we will be going to the property to investigate soon after the hunting season ends. I will be spending a great deal of time in the woods there in the next few weeks armed with a camera and I plan to spend extra time scouting for evidence of bigfoot when I'm not hunting.

Third report - December 30th, 2009 08:25 PM

Update to original post; Went to the hunting property for three days this past weekend. My parents and my son spent four days... nothing too much to report. I couldn't get to the big creek bottom where most of the "monkey" sounds were coming from that the others had heard. The road going in was bad due to the excessive rainfall of last week. I did get fairly close on one day and found some rather strange tracks in the creek bed. I showed my son that there were three distinct toes coming off of a slender track but it was very hard to tell what to make of it since they were partly in the mud and partly in the leaves. There were rather large foot-shaped areas in the boggy area that were filled in with water. The unusual thing was the stride was about four to five feet. It would be very hard for a human to accomplish without slipping down in that bottom.

Forest Friends of the Night

There was also a skinny pine tree about twenty feet high that was bent toward the ground without being broken. No other tree in the vicinity was that way. We had no sounds at all from where we were. I did hear distinctly the sounds of owls many times.

Fourth report - Posted: January 10th, 2010 02:11 PM

My son and I met with the investigator in the Columbus, Georgia area. We had a good talk over coffee that lasted quite a while. As far as any updates, not too much happened over the last four days of hunting. I did find a tree about two inches in diameter that had been completely twisted and broken about six to seven feet

off the ground. I didn't have my camera that evening due to the batteries being dead from the cold, but I will go back and get some photos next week.

My son had one interesting shot on a trail cam at night. It showed eye shine from of deer in a food plot and a red eye shine behind them of an unknown being about seven feet above ground level. It appeared to be about fifty yards or so beyond them at the edge of the woods. My son's camera was set to catch movement and with the wind he had more than eighteen hundred photos and in an attempt to delete the unwanted portion, he deleted them all.

He did remember another unique photo he had saved from last summer in the fog that was something rather strange and definitely not a deer. We will forward that photo to the investigator soon. We plan to return many times after the season to camp and continue looking. We will take the BFRO investigator with us as occasion permits.

Fifth report - January 15th, 2010 10:13 PM
Just got home from our hunting property and we have spent seven days of the last two weeks in the woods there. I used the new knowledge learned here and have gathered some new evidence!

I concentrated a lot of time looking for the tree twists or breaks and found many in the creek bottoms. Most of them are small hardwood trees that have been bent over and either broken or broken and twisted. Many are seven feet or more above the ground. There is no way I or anyone else I know could bend these and break them at that height. I know it is not wind damage. If this were the wind causing this, it would not be a situation where one tree is bent none surrounding it are harmed.

Forest Friends of the Night

My parents heard some very weird screams and deep guttural noises. Today, after a deer hunt where there was a deer shot and field dressed, they heard the scream like sound in a sequence of three from that area. No one would go back down there to check it out as it was slightly unnerving. My dad has hunted for fifty years and the sounds we have heard lately are unlike any he has ever heard. Unfortunately, today, when Mom and Dad heard them, I was on another section of our property so didn't hear them.

*Sixth Report - January 20th, 2010 9PM

I write this from my hotel room in Harlington TX.

Mom, Dad and son are camping on our hunting property. Deer hunting season is now closed. My son likes to camp and coyote hunt just before turkey season starts in the spring. We have a large population of coyotes and they real hurt our deer and turkey populations. On this evening, I received a frantic call from their Onstar in Dad's truck. The conversation was pretty exciting! My son was out of breath, as he tells me, "You are NOT GOING TO BELIEVE WHAT HAPPENED"... I do want to say here, my son is sixteen in a few days and he is a large kid... an inch over six feet and weighing just less than 200 pounds... he doesn't scare very easily. I asked him to tell me the story...

He had been coyote hunting in the late afternoon and early evening. It was later in the day when he heard the gorilla/monkey sound that had been heard so many times. He felt it was not far from where he is hunting and he was approximately a quarter mile from where we camped. He decided he would return to camp after hearing this since it was but a few minutes before dark. He walked back to camp and told my parents what he had heard.

He was outside walking their little dog and heard noises in the woods close to camp and heard coyotes howl only about a hundred yards away. He put the dog back in the camper and decided to take his shotgun loaded with buckshot and a flashlight to the other side of camp where he shined it down a long logging road. He was hoping he could get a shot at the coyotes but he couldn't see anything. He did hear a rustling in the thick underbrush beside him. It sounded like it is about fifty yards from him and was walking straight toward him. While he was trying to decide if it was a coyote, he realized it was much too large. When he heard a very loud crack of a stick being stepped on and broken, he realized the truth of this. As the noise got closer, he began to see the trees parting and shaking as whatever it was came toward him. He shined the light toward the sound thinking that if it is an animal it will freeze and stop the advance. He also raised his shotgun and pointed it toward the sound. As soon as he did that, his subject ran straight toward him making a terrible racket! He was terrified and began running back into the light of camp.

Forest Friends of the Night

The creature stopped at the edge of the tree line and turned, walking around camp then heading behind the campers in a direction away from my son. He said it was very dark, but he could make out the movement as it walked completely out of hearing. He said he could hear an occasional snap of a stick as it walked away. He then ran into the camper told my parents about what had happened.

The only animal I have known that would charge like that was a wild hog and we have never seen one on our property. So, was it a bigfoot?

*Seventh Report - February 7th 2010

We drove to our hunting property to take another game camera down. It was intended to be a quick trip and we were only going to be there long enough to check our cameras hanging there and to set up another.

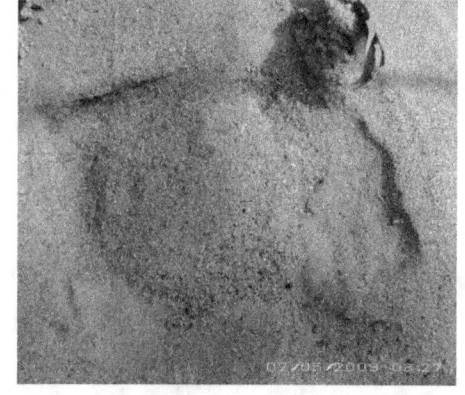

On our arrival, we were disappointed to learn one of the cameras appeared to have been turned off. We didn't get any good pictures form this device and the other only had deer. We decided to take this camera to the creek where all of the

Forest Friends of the Night

Gorilla/monkey sounds were usually heard. As we moved to the creek, we found a human like track on the sandbar of the creek. You could very clearly make out the shape of the right foot with a deep heel impression. The toes were not well defined because of the sandy texture but you could see they were there. The track measured thirteen inches long and six inches wide, smaller than what I have always thought a track would be. Using the standard anatomical conversion a thirteen inch track would indicate a primate's height to be just over seven feet in height. The area of the foot would indicate a weight of just under six hundred pounds. We took photos and a video of it. We also found a couple more tree breaks and some trees bent over forming arches along a very well

defined trail paralleling the creek. We set up the camera along the creek where a very good game trail crossed and we then made our way back to the truck for our drive home.

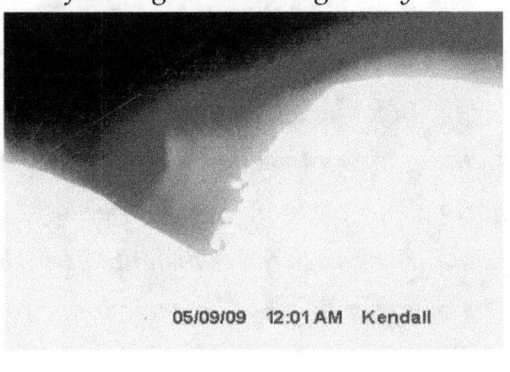

05/09/09   12:01 AM   Kendall

Subsequent investigation of the hundreds of game camera pictures revealed a couple I felt worth sending to the BFRO investigator a closer look. The most interesting photograph had something so close to the camera on a night shot, the flash turned the image completely white with a weird red aura around it. It resembled a head with hair and shoulders visible. This picture was taken during the week when no one was there and the gate locked.

Eighth Report - March 19, 2010

We had some interesting activity last Friday night. We arrived Friday night about ten pm and we have been the only ones on the property for two weeks. We were combining turkey hunting with further bigfoot investigations.

My son had a new red dot scope installed on his turkey gun and wanted to shoot in in order to sight it in. I placed a target for him that could be illuminated by my truck headlights and he shot a few times. When he finished we continued unloading our gear to get ready for bed. About ten minutes after we had finished sighting his gun, we heard a very clear distinct bird whistle just north of our camp that was quite close. It was probably no more than fifty or sixty yards distant. The whistle emanated from a section of scrub oaks that encircle our camp.

It has places that are impenetrable, but this area can be walked easily on the many game trails. It is located approximately two hundred yards from our deer feeder and food plots. We put these in after the season to help the deer through the winter and the time of low food growth. It attracts all animals so this area is full of wildlife.

Forest Friends of the Night

This "bird call" sound was similar to a dove's loud mating coo but was long and drawn out with reverberations in the tone. However, I know doves do not call in the middle of the night as they are on roost making this something out of the ordinary.

A few minutes later we heard a whoop, loudly, clearly and distinctly. It came from between the area of the birdcall and the feeder/food plot area. We heard a reply from the opposite side of the camp toward the big creek bottom.

A few minutes later we heard owl calls coming from two separate places. These sounded like barn owls and were very clear but, about five minutes later, a loud "sick owl" sounded off and set off a barrage of coyote calls from very close range.

My son was getting unnerved at this time and he and I were both straining our ears to hear any footfalls. We began to hear the leaves rustling behind my camper. I was pretty sure it was some sort of animal other than our bigfoot friends because the rustling was way too loud and not the carefully placed footfalls we normally hear. After a nervous minute, my son finally spotted the culprit. An Armadillo was shuffling through the leaves. We affectionately call them possums on the half shell. After a few more minutes, it settled down and we got to bed with relief as it is getting close to midnight and we were both tired from the trip.

Forest Friends of the Night

Around six thirty am, my son banged on my camper door. He had been sleeping in my parent's camper while I was in ours. He woke me from a sound sleep and when he came in, he asked "Did you hear that?"

I told him "No, you woke me up."

He said he heard a very loud scream that made all of the hair stand up on his neck. He waited a few minutes until it got daylight then he went outside as I stood there at the door.

"I smelled a terrible odor like very rotten eggs or rotting meat. It was coming from the area where the whoops and the bird sound we heard had come from. About ten minutes later, it was completely gone. He then headed off to his turkey hunt and I laid back down for a couple more winks before getting up to make coffee.

Later that morning, after the turkey hunt, we decided to check all of the game cameras and retrieved more than seven hundred pictures to evaluate. After a ride to town and a good late breakfast, we returned for an approximately two mile trek looking for sign. The BFRO investigator that was working with us texted me to state she was enroute and would arrive that night between seven and eight pm. We concentrated the first part of our day on searching for sign in the creek bottoms.

Forest Friends of the Night

In that search, we discovered something I thought is very different... piles of defecate on rocks in the creek! One that aroused our interest we found on a rock about three feet high. The diameter of the defecate was not as large as that we found earlier at the deer kill, but definitely was not the size that would be left by a raccoon, coyote or other smaller animal. It was very dark... almost black in color, indicating a large amount of ingested blood was present. We then worked our way downstream and found two more places about a hundred yards apart that were the same way. One was on a large flat rock pile that is adjacent to an embankment. The orientation of this one, like all of them we found, indicated the being that made them was in the creek itself. I told my son to dig around in the waste to see if he could find any hair, seeds, or other identifiable vegetation. He found that to be the case as hair, seeds of some sort and a fibrous like substance were present therein. So, this is from an animal that eats both meat and plants. The only animal that we have here exhibits this behavior is the fox but I have never seen foxes swim into a creek expressly to defecate on a rock.

After covering enough ground to have lost a couple of pounds walking (much needed), we had covered at least two thirds of the creeks and had found nothing in the way of tracks but we did find a couple of broken trees and a stick structure. We returned to camp late in the afternoon so I told Kendall that, after a rest, we would take a look around the camp.

Forest Friends of the Night

We walked a circle about a hundred yards out from camp where we immediately found a hardwood tree that had pretty large limbs broken and pulled straight down. They were wedged in some thick briars. We then found another just past the first one with some limbs broken over ten feet off the ground! One tree was broken in half. This is in the area where the bluff charge had occurred. We walked over to the area where the first whoop/bird call had come from and we found a very fresh scrub oak broken and twisted down in exactly the same way. That this one had been extremely recent was evident from the green leaves still on the tree.

The BFRO investigator arrived around eight pm... after dark. We took some flashlights down to the creek bottom and I showed her the structure made of sticks. She pointed out the fact there were new limbs that have leaves mixed with the old branches indicating the new limbs are being added to the already formed structure. She also pointed out a lean-to type structure where a fallen tree and limbs were forming a little shelter in the treetop. I didn't get photos because it was dark and I had left my camera at camp.

Forest Friends of the Night

The BFRO investigator was ready to head back to camp and start a fire. I did show her the tree breaks at camp, which she found very interesting. We sat next to a fire and listened for sounds. We heard coyotes a few times and then we heard the bird whistle. I knew this was no bird I had ever heard here before beside the point that it was dark and they were all roosting.

I asked her if that was a bird, she responded by saying she thought so, but she had no idea what it was. I told her that was no bird I have ever heard in the tirty years we have had the land.

I had also showed her a spot next to the stick structure where a deer had been caught. The hair was pulled out in large clumps with skin attached.

We sat there until fairly late and the firewood began to run low. At that time the BFRO investigator left for home and we headed to bed.

*9th report - March 28, 2010
Last Friday night the whoops and screams seemed like they were everywhere. Then Saturday arrived and nothing occurred. There was nothing this weekend either. The wind blew the entire weekend but I have no idea if that was the reason or not.

Forest Friends of the Night

There were many, many new tree breaks... and another surprise... a stick structure that had been built since last weekend.

We also found a deer leg bone lying in the creek in the area where we find most of the evidence of tracks, tree breaks, bent trees, deer bones and the dead deer we found killed a few weeks ago. The trees we found were all saplings or just a bit bigger. They were bent and twisted with some torn completely apart. We tried to break a couple of trees of the same size and species where these have been found. We can't even begin to break them this way. The most we can do is bend the smaller of them.

10 Report- April 11 2010

We had some very interesting activity this weekend! We had some great vocalizations which were not recorded because I had forgotten my digital recorder! This was a weekend for turkey hunting and bigfoot investigation on our property.

We left Friday after work and my son was in such a hurry to leave, he packed everything and I forgot to ask about the recorder until we got to our destination. Of course, the best activity we have gotten for vocalizations in a few months occurred and all we had were cell phones and my blackberry. We recorded using these but you can't hear anything of value except the coyotes who got stirred up afterwards.

Forest Friends of the Night

We had howl/scream sounds around dusk then again around nine thirty pm. They started at the low end of the register like a cow then the tone rose and got higher and maintained the same note for many seconds. We placed this one about a half mile away and down toward the swamp area. This vocalization was immediately answered by the same sound in front of us. It was probably about the same distance away from us as the original vocalization. It sent chills up my spine!

I asked my son to describe to me what it sounded like to him and he said, "... The sound is like what would be on television in a Hollywood manufactured ghost sound. It was like, oooohhhhhhhhhhaaaaaaaaahhhhh." That was what it reminded him of... just ten times louder. That, to me, was a pretty apt description.

The coyotes went out of control over this and were all around us barking and braying. The woods seemed alive with sounds, and standing next to a fire barrel with no lights, it was very unnerving, even for a big guy like me. I was brought up as an avid outdoorsman that would not even sleep in a camper until a few years ago. Age kind of creeped up on me making me realize there are some things I might have to change a bit as comfort now takes precedence over much in my life.

Forest Friends of the Night

A few minutes after the coyotes finally calmed, my son decided to whistle. His whistle was then promptly answered by a short version (three seconds or so) of the same sound as we had heard before. I then tried the whistle and was answered promptly! We did this back and forth for four or five more times before it finally stopped.

Around eleven pm it got pretty quiet so we decided to call it a night and head for bed. I was wakened about three am by noises just outside my camper. It sounded like three distinct knocking sounds. It had to be in camp or very close.

We arose at five thirty am and were standing outside when the burnt orange globe of the sun made its appearance on the horizon. We heard another scream/howl down near the swamp area a half mile distant. Again the coyotes went ballistic, but on the opposite side of the property. This made me wish for a parabolic microphone and some better equipment.

I received some bad news today. We have lost our hunting lease and this weekend's investigation will be the last one. It is very difficult to know we have hunted and camped on this property for over thirty years and it ends this weekend. We had some really extraordinary things happen here, too. I sure hope we can have some this weekend. It would be great to have some good stuff to share with everyone.

Forest Friends of the Night

I did want to relate something I thought strange. I am not saying that this is necessarily related to bigfoot, it could just be happenstance... We had placed a camera on the stick structure about a month ago or so. We have been down there every week to check it and every single time there is a problem. Sometimes the camera is flashing an error code with the card. Another time the batteries, which were right out of the box new, were inexplicably discharged... Maybe the flash didn't work... We even tried changing cameras twice. We have thousands of pictures from all of the cameras in different places but not even one from that camera which was located on the stick structure!

6. A New Start

This new season brought a new start for me. The property that had been our hunting lease for so long was gone and we had to find new land to hunt on. We joined a club that a friend of mine had leased for over twenty years. I was a bit sad that we were not on my familiar lease but the chance of being in a new area I had never hunted was exciting. It was also an hour closer to my house so instead of being a little over two hours, I could be there in just one. The first trip there in the late summer to look at the property was exciting. I was also a bit relieved there was no sign of broken or bent trees or anything else that would indicate there could be a possible bigfoot type creature there. I was still a bit concerned about my son being in the woods by himself because of that.

This season was new and as it progressed I saw nothing that appeared odd. We didn't hear any of the usual vocals and the strange sounds in the night as we did at the other lease about eighty miles south of this location.

As we ended the deer season and with turkey season nearing, we made another trip down to ready the camp. We were cutting grass, getting the campers in place and putting up blinds to get the season started. As we were erecting the blinds, I saw a tree bowed over in an area I had hunted for deer a few weeks earlier.

I wondered if bigfoot was here as well. I decided maybe this was simply a random event. Possibly an All-Terrain Vehicle had ran over the tree. We would kick off the turkey season the following weekend and this property had a much higher population of turkeys than the other location did... that would be fun. With this in mind, I determined to not let what might be disturb what actually is. We drove home that night and the anticipation was high for the new turkey season.

I contacted, via e-mail, the lady from the BFRO that had helped us and thanked her for all of her help. I told her that I thought we were in a location now that would not need her expertise. She then told me stories of sightings within a mile or two of our property. Many of those were near the Chattahoochee River that was about two miles from this property. Of course, this concerned me some, but I also felt a bit glad that I might be able to still learn about these "animals". I still wanted to verify one hundred percent that they were real.

7. The Unwanted Visitors

We arrived in camp the very late on the Friday evening before turkey season. My wife, my son and I immediately noticed our camper windows had been smashed out! Our hearts sank over the thought of someone breaking into our camper. Upon investigation, it was evident the camper had been ransacked as many articles of clothing. A hunting bow and many other items were gone. We then noticed another camper next to ours was also broken into. There were televisions, compact disc players and other things taken. I called the fellow hunter and told him what had happened, and then called the local Sheriff's department to report it.

As the deputy sheriff pulled up, the entire area was lit with blue lights. The deputy got out of his car and seemed pretty nervous. I thought perhaps it was because we were located in a remote area, surrounded by woods and it was ten o'clock at night. I met him at his car as he got out and we walked towards the camper. The entire time he was peering intently into the woods with his hand on his holstered gun. As we got to within ten feet of the wood line, he pulled his gun while still looking into the woods. At the same time, I heard a stick break and he told me he thought a person dressed in black was back there.

I stood beside him at that point, afraid to move. Approximately five minutes later, he put his gun back into the holster and said, "Maybe my eyes were playing tricks on me". I however did hear a stick break, so I am thought it could have been an animal of some sort just startled by all of the commotion.

We filled out the police report and tried to tidy up the camper as best we could. I had a portable drill and screws in my truck so I used some galvanized metal we had laying at camp and sealed up the two windows that were broken out. We swept up the glass and went to bed.

The next morning, my son left to go hunting and I stayed at camp because my wife was too nervous to be left alone. When I awoke, I got dressed and walked out to look around. I found it interesting to see some of the trees at the edge of camp were bowed over with a couple of them snapped off. One tree was broken about four feet off the ground and the tree top lay parallel to the camper along the wood line. There was a small ravine that ran all the way up to that area and it appeared there was a very well used path along the ravine to where the tree top was. Could the ones that broke into the camper have used this trail to spy on the campers? That really didn't make too much sense because the road was the opposite direction. The ravine went towards a very thick area of the woods and as I walked down this trail, there were many trees bowed and it created a tunnel effect. This brought to mind the same type of bent trees back at our prior lease. As I returned to camp, I wondered, could the bigfoot be here?

When I approached the camp, I noticed a black sedan pulling in. I walked up to meet a detective that had come to talk with us regarding the break in. He had with him a game camera and he placed it in the same area of the bent over trees adjacent to the camper. He told me, "Somebody has been standing around that pushed over tree. The trail shows places where they have walked up here in the pine straw."

I looked and sure enough there were imprints there. I thought to myself, those are some big foot print impressions.

8. Tricksters in the Woods

The next weekend we headed to our camp on Friday night. Turkey season has been a little slow and the last weekend's excitement prevented me from being able to do much hunting. This weekend, I hoped for a less stressful time. As we arrived at camp, nothing seemed out of order so we just prepared a quick meal and went to bed.

The alarm clock slowly roused me from a deep sleep. I got up and stumbled into the camper kitchen to start coffee. We had been promised great weather and I was excited to get out and see the sunrise. As I got the ATV going, I let it run for a minute then started down the ATV trail to my area. About a third of the way from camp to my destination, I entered a long stand if pines. The pines grew in long, straight rows. There were almost no other types of tree because the property was leased to us by a timber company that grows the trees for lumber. They clear out four foot areas to the side of each stand, then a ten foot row between them. A person can see a long way between these rows.

As I got just inside the pines, I could see a tree blocking the ATV trail. It was not a big tree and with a bit of effort, I slid it far enough out of the way for me to get by. Then it occurred to me... this is a small hardwood tree. There are NO hardwood trees anywhere close to these pines. It certainly was not there the weekend before! Scratching my head, I continued driving down that path to my hunting area.

For about an hour, I was being entertained by the gobbles of tom turkeys. I spent a little time talking back to them with my hen calls. I was able to call a couple of the birds in close and was having a grand time with the hunt. I was sitting quietly, listening for another gobble, when I heard a large CRASH! It was the sound of a tree falling and it was so close that it startled me! After a while, hunger pangs got too much for me to endure, so I walked to the ATV and headed back to camp.

About fifty yards down the trail, I noticed another tree blocking my path! This one was substantially bigger so I had to use my ATV to pull it enough to unblock my path. I always keep a tow rope the ATV for those situations. I looked at the tree closely and saw that was a pine and appeared to be dead. This one I chalked up to coincidence.

I arrived back at camp in good shape. After lunch, I headed back to the opposite side of the property. I parked my ATV a few yards down a trail and out of sight and walked to a small field to set up some turkey decoys I had brought with me. After completing that, I settled into my new spot. There was dense vegetation that I had to clear in order to make an area for me to sit. It made a very good natural blind.

I was sitting there waiting on things to settle down a bit when I heard bird whistle I did not know. It was a very loud whistle with a bit of a shrill to it that I had never heard before. It continued for a very long duration before it stopped. It paused for two or three minutes before starting over. I was intrigued. I was thinking deeply, trying to determine what kind of bird it could possibly be. It seemed to be only about fifty or sixty yards distant, across the field just inside the edge of the forest. After thirty minutes of this, I was beginning to get annoyed hearing this sound. I finally stood up and walked over to the edge of the field. When I got there, I saw nothing, but the whistling stopped. I stood there for a few minutes before returning to my blind.

As soon as I begin walking back across the field, the whistling began again. This time, however, it was deeper in the woods that were paralleled by an old logging road. I skirted the edge of the field and got to the logging road because the walking would be easier there. I was moving slowly while trying to locate this irritating bird! I stopped once I got close to where the sound was and, again, it sounded further away. I had decided I would only walk a little farther and I assumed if I scared it far enough from my hunting area, I would be well off.

As I stopped to listen for it to sound off again, I was standing in front of a pile of rather large rocks. They were stacked up and they were arranged so I knew it had to have been done by a hand. Some of the rocks were very large and it would have

taken considerable strength to put them where they were.
My initial thought was WHY would someone do that? What
is it for? If not for the bird, I would not have found it
although it was located on the side of the logging trail that I
and others drive often.

I was thoroughly perplexed by this so I simply went
back to the field, got my decoys and drove back to camp. I
told my wife Cathy about it and how strange it was.

She asked. "Does Bigfoot do that stuff?"

I told her, "Well I guess they could." The more I
thought about the things that had happened, the more I
began to think maybe they did.

The next morning, my son and I switched sides of the
property. He drove down the side I had hunted the prior
morning. He drove by the fallen trees and I went to the
other side. I saw a couple of jakes (first year young toms)
and nothing else. Nothing unusual happened at all.

My son arrived in camp just a few minutes after me.
We exchanged stories of the morning hunt then he said, "I
had to drag a little hardwood tree out of the trail on the way
down."

I asked him, "Was it actually across the trail?"

He replied, "Yes, why?"

I simply told him, "I thought I had it far enough out of the trail yesterday."

It was then that I KNEW something was messing with us. This was confirmed for sure the next weekend when the tree was back across the trail. This time I actually moved it by dragging it several hundred feet away.

9. Guidance and Discovery

In the last few weeks, I have begun a campaign of discovery. I have "researched" answers to my activity. I have joined forums on the internet about Bigfoot and other mysteries. In joining these forums, I found a few to be totally accepting of me and I began posting and asking questions. Some answers made sense, others did not. I began to notice there were more opinions than answers. I decided to use the few folks that seemed to make sense and concentrate on them to help me. I looked a few up on Facebook and was very fortunate to be introduced to people like Arla Williams, Alex Midnight Walker and Thom Cantrall. I also met Autumn Williams through a forum and she even reached out to me by phone. She called me one day and helped answer questions for a very long time. The answers to my questions began to start making sense!

A few people were now really helping me understand. Arla Williams spent many hours instructing me in things to do when out in the woods. She became my "rock" and many hours of discussion endeared me to this wonderful woman. I also had many discussions with my "editor" of this book, Thom Cantrall. He was also friends with Arla and the understanding he had of these fascinating people helped me overcome my fear of what they are. I began to hear them referred to as "Primal People" not monsters. Slowly but surely my level of understanding has increased. I was now looking forward to my next camping trip to try a few things I learned!

On a Friday evening in the spring, we packed up the truck and headed back to the property. This time, we had our grandson, Lane, with us. We drove down and just went to bed soon after arriving as it was so late. Lane, who was four at the time, slept with us in the camper that first night. Cathy and I were still awake and whispering because we didn't want to disturb Lane, who was fast asleep.

As we turned over to go to sleep, I heard a noise right outside the camper. Cathy asked me; "what was that?"

I replied that I didn't know and I was listening intently. After a few minutes had passed, I was almost asleep when I heard the sound of talking outside the camper. There was no one due into camp that night and the gate was closed and locked. I became a bit nervous because of the break-in a couple of weeks earlier. We had installed motion lights, but none were on. I then heard what I can best describe as gibberish... almost like another language. It was loud enough that Cathy heard it as well. I instantly just knew….they are here! There are bigfoot outside!

I told Cathy, "They are here! They are outside!" There was a few seconds more of the gibberish-like talk, sounding low and deep, and then there was silence... I had absolutely no fear, just wonderment of what we heard. I lay awake for just a while before finally entering into a very deep sleep.

I awoke in the morning feeling wonderful. The sleep had been very restful and, for whatever reason, I was just happy! I skipped going out to hunt turkey and just made some coffee and stepped outside to watch the morning wake up. It was a beautifully cool spring morning with a glorious sunrise. I was the first one up and wanted to catch these first few moments of the  day alone. I felt totally connected with everything. I decided I wanted to drive down the four wheeler trail that had been blocked by the tree week earlier.

Forest Friends of the Night

As I drove around the corner from camp, I noticed a young pine tree that had been bent all the way over until the top was touching the ground. I thought it looked odd and I knew it wasn't that way last weekend. I got off the ATV and walked over to take a look. At that point, it became even MORE amazing! There was an older dead tree that had been lying in the grass a few feet away. That tree had been moved and placed on the top of the branches, pinning it to the ground! This was a large, dead tree that would have taken enormous strength to move and the tree was an estimated thirty feet tall. I stood there scratching my head... That was an amazing sight.

I drove back to camp to share this with Cathy and Lane when they woke up. As I entered the camper, they were both up eating a breakfast consisting of doughnuts and a cola. Cathy knew I was excited to share something so I told her about the tree and they hurriedly got dressed and we headed

out to see. Since it was only about a hundred yards from camp, we walked the distance.

On this particular trip we had a big day planned with Lane. One of the things Arla had told me was that if you want to improve your chances of connecting with the bigfoot people in your area, just have fun. If there are kids there, laugh, play and enjoy yourselves. They really enjoy watching people have fun... so we did just that. We ate watermelon and had a picnic. We then rode the ATV down to the area where the rock stack was located. We left them a slice of watermelon on the big rock and we talked to them to tell them who we were. We explained to Lane they were just forest friends and they lived in the woods. He began yelling, "Hello friends, we left you a gift!" After a few minutes, we returned to camp.

That evening we grilled outside and sat by the fire for a while. We began to hear rumbles of thunder and the wind picked up as some springtime thunder storms blew in, so we ended up going inside earlier than we had expected.

By morning, the storms had ended and the skies were clearing. We had nothing happen with all of the rain from the night before and Lane's mother was on her way to retrieve him.

Forest Friends of the Night

My step-daughter, Amanda, only lived a few miles away. So, we got Lane packed up and Amanda arrived around ten am so we went out to open the gate and greet her. The morning was cool but warming a bit from the evening before. Amanda was standing next to her car talking to us. Cathy was facing Amanda and I was beside Amanda talking to Lane as he was already in the car in his child's seat. A couple of minutes later, I noticed Cathy straining to look over Amanda's shoulder towards the woods. She kept glancing at me then back to Amanda. I knew she had seen something and I looked towards the woods, but saw nothing. In the meantime, Amanda had been preoccupied with Lane's bag and was putting it into the car. My wife had a very puzzled and shocked look on her face, but changed her demeanor as soon as Amanda turned back around to tell her goodbye with a hug. After I said my goodbyes and got my hugs, we watched them drive out with the final waves as they went through the gate. Cathy then turned to me very excited and said, "I SAW ONE!!

I was a bit surprised, thinking at first she meant a deer or turkey. I asked, "Saw what?"

"A bigfoot!"

I asked, "Where was he?"

Forest Friends of the Night

"Right over there near that dead tree that was pushed over! It peaked around that tree and looked at me!"

I asked, "What did it look like?"

She replied, "A big, hairy man with a dark colored face and dark brown hair!" She told me she didn't want to scare Lane or Amanda so she didn't say anything.

I walked to the area and couldn't find any tracks. I stood beside the tree and asked her how high was it?

She told me, "Its head was at the bottom of the limb that was about two feet higher than my head."

I am six feet and an inch so that would have made it around eight feet tall! Now I was very excited and the first thing I could think of was what Arla had told me, "just have fun and they will connect with you if they want to!"

Needless to say, my wife and I were extremely excited! A visual and another fantastic discovery of the bigfoot people.

10. Realization and Reality

The next few days left me in a daze. I could think of nothing else for a long time. Cathy actually seemed to cope with it better than I did. I think because of all of the past things I have heard and experienced, the validity finally just hit me between the eyes.

Yes, I saw prints and yes, I saw glimpses of what I couldn't identify, but now it was verified and the feelings were overwhelming me. I had hundreds of questions. Exactly what are they? Where did they come from? How do they hide so well? I had so many questions!

I then began to immerse myself into as much information as I could find. I joined many Facebook groups and I continued posting on the forum of which I was part. Meanwhile, I kept going camping and looking for sign of them... It seemed there was a lot of sign.

Seeing other people's posts of tree bows, "X" formations, structures of all kinds and rock stacks, I began taking photos which I would send to others to peruse to help me understand. I began to notice subtleties that helped me know there were not naturally occurring situations. I was in controlled entry situations most of the time. At our hunting camp, only a few people could get past the gate.

I began trying to understand the references to the Native people. Hearing my friends Arla, Thom and others discussing the Native American views, I learned the bigfoot people were integral in so much history of not only Native Americans, but Native people all over the world. There were pictures of them dating back many hundreds of years.

There was one that particularly captivated me in an area named Painted Rock. It is located on the Tule

River Indian Reservation in the Sierra Nevada foothills of central California. The pictograph there is called "Hairy Man" and shows what was described as huge, hairy men that were the subject of many tribal stories. It is a very

profound bit of history.

There was a lady I had met on the forum, whose name is Kathy Strain who was very knowledgeable in this area. She has shared volumes of great information regarding the area and the drawings found there.

Another thing I learned quickly was how completely disrespectful people could be when it came to this subject. Probably due to the years of the bigfoot people being stereotyped, many simply thought it was a myth like

Forest Friends of the Night

Santa Claus or Leprechauns... just something made up. I wanted to tell things that had happened, but simply could not. Some would ridicule me for just talking about it. Some of my own family, even, would laugh at the mere mention of bigfoot. I became very selective of whom I would even discuss this. I was taught very quickly the "bigfoot community" had people that would rip one apart if you discussed some aspects. It seems as though the entire subject was highly emotionally charged.

The ones I began to trust quickly became my sole source for questions and answers. In many ways, they kept me sane by being there to help me understand. They were very valuable in my understanding. I often feel if it were not for them, I would have just simply given up. Being made fun of was very upsetting to me at first, but eventually I became somewhat used to it... except for my family members who were making fun of me... I don't think I will ever forget that.

I received some reports that I thought I should include here. While I have changed or left out the names to protect identities, the stories are reproduced with total accuracy.

Margaret's Story - *1/28/2010*

This account was a result of someone sharing my story and this was sent back in return:

Dear Margaret,

Thanks for the email about bigfoot. It is very interesting. I will reply more fully in time, but have run out of that time today. From what I have read, it seems like a bigfoot to me, also. I have also heard their screams and it sounds just like the background monkey screams you used to hear on the old Tarzan movies. Their screams were so fierce it made you feel safe and cozy just to be inside the house. I would hear their screams at two or three am.

One time, I heard it screaming at a dog and the dog would then bark wildly. It would scream again, and back and forth they would go several times. It was close to our house and I would lay awake at night and hear it scream sometimes. That was when I had injured my back, and didn't sleep well at night. Now I wear ear plugs, and don't hear anything.

Macland Road - 1/28/2010

Forest Friends of the Night

"I couldn't make out the last picture as it is too dark. What was the red in the third picture?

I used to go in the woods a lot when my boys were young. We went to deer camp with them but I never thought about looking at trees like that. That was few year. back.

My youngest son & his dad hunt in south Georgia a lot but I don't remember what county. I have heard enough stories for this area too.

When my boys were little we went to visit friends who lived on Macland Road which was close to the county line. There was a creek and swampy area behind their house where my boys and the friend's kids all played every time we visited. One day, my children refused to go out and the other kids said it was because they saw bigfoot near the creek. They never would go back out there to play.

What gets me is, where do they go? I have thoughts, of course... maybe underground? ... Maybe another dimension? I know that sounds weird, but I kind of believe in that too. (Like in the Bermuda triangle.)

Anyway thanks for the pictures and PLEASE let me know what they say about this last incident."

Donna's Story

Forest Friends of the Night

I met Donna on the forum and, after many discussions, we exchanged e-mails. She was a biologist and also had an interest in bigfoot because of things that she experienced. This is an account of her first encounter that she chose to share with me: Donna wrote...

"I have another new friend interested in what I've had going on here, so I thought I'd share this with both of you. This is my best visual and my first encounter. At least, as an adult...

This location is a place I go when I've decided "it's a nice night, I think I'll ride out to the country and sit a while." I never plan it in advance so the chance of someone hoaxing us there is slim and none. This is where I had my first sighting and became obsessed.

Hubby and I had had one of those mandatory married people spats and I decided to go for a drive... maybe sleep at my sister's place in the boonies. I'd been reading some of the stuff about bigfoot recently.

My brother had shown up the day the Georgia Boy's hoax hit the net and showed me the pics. I looked at the teeth and told him I was sorry to burst his bubble but those teeth didn't belong to a primate and if bigfoot was real, he was a primate.

Forest Friends of the Night

I'd spent my whole life with this brother trying to scare me with monster stories. Maybe that's why I still don't scare easily? He turned me on to (Professor Jeff) Meldrum. Knowing my background, he knew someone peer reviewed would be the best way to get my attention. I started digging for myself... I had thought the Patterson-Gimlin Film had been proven a hoax. Looking at the new stabilized version was enlightening. I started to think maybe they did exist in the PNW.

I started listening to some of the sounds. Until hearing chatter for myself I questioned the Sierra Sounds. Now I know it had to be real. What we heard sounded like the same language with different word and a voice not as deep with a different tone altogether. Then I found some of the screams. I had heard them twice in my teens and had wondered about them since. (One associated with what I call the "owl on acid riding a sick cow") At that point I decided they might be real and maybe they were around here way back, but not anymore. I did check Google Maps and realized there is a good chunk of available habitat near my sister and the wildlife corridors they've been establishing throughout the state are really coming together.

I found myself by-passing my sister's place and deciding to ride out and sit by the river instead. It was a full moon, cloudless, still night. When I got there I figured according to the maps, I was in prime habitat. I pulled over and just sat a little while before deciding that since no one was around, I could go ahead and be a dufus. I'd go ahead and knock and try a whoop.

I sat awhile, just enjoying the night and started hearing something in the brush across the street. I thought I heard whispers but discounted it as a breeze in the weeds or some little critter scratching around over there. I was looking forward and something in my peripheral vision caught my attention. I looked directly across the road and saw a silhouette of a head and the left shoulder poking out from behind a tree trunk. It looked to be about my size. I'm five feet two inches. It did have a visible neck and a round little head. I think, because of the slightness of the build it was probably a juvenile female... Adolescent age, perhaps.

I was trying to make sense of it. It looked like it was only a few feet off the ground. I thought it must be an illusion so I tried all the tricks, including scrunching my eyes... shut to deform the lens and force a refocus several times. Then I stared at it, trying to will it to move. ...Nothing... I thought I saw something in my peripheral vision flash across the road where it started to bend behind the truck. Whatever it was was on all fours and moving much like a gorilla with a high butt. We don't have bears around here... Haven't for decades and certainly none that big had ever lived here. It was across the road and gone so fast that was all the impression I got.

Forest Friends of the Night

I turned my head to try to see what it was and when I looked back the little head and shoulder were gone... No branch, no nothing but the straight trunk of the tree in sharp outline under the full moon behind it. I was sitting there, looking for an explanation when I got a prickly feeling and joked with myself "here you are staring across the road, you'll turn around and there will be a big face smashed up against the window." I was very, very relieved and laughed at myself when there wasn't.

I kept turning and looked out the back door window. Twenty to thirty feet away, in the shadows, behind and over a palmetto about five to six feet tall was a face. All I could see of it was the moonlight reflecting off the bare skin. Everything else was in shadows. I have a black lambskin coat, and the skin had the same soft, supple appearance of that leather. I assume the reflection stopped where the hairlines began. I saw heavy supra-orbital arches, not a straight brow ridge. He had very high, broad cheekbones. There was a little reflection where either the chin or mouth would be, but it was very hard to tell.

A large, wide, fleshy nose was evident. I'm not sure why I didn't immediately dub him Jimmy, as in Durante due to that nose. I expected a nose more like a gorilla... This wasn't making any sense.

I repeated the routine while looking at the face... forcing my eyes to refocus, checking around in the truck for something that could be reflecting inside the windows, making sure it wasn't just a pattern of leaves and branches... I scrunched my brows a little and squinted at it. The response was the only motion I saw and I'm not a hundred percent sure I didn't imagine it but it appeared the face squinted right back at me!

Something bounced off the road and skipped across behind me. It had the sharp crack of a pebble and seemed to skip across more than bounce from a fall. It could have been an acorn falling, but it didn't sound like it. I turned to look and saw nothing. I looked back for the face and it was gone. There was not so much as a clump of leaves... just empty, black space.

I sat there pondering it for a little while as I watched and listened. Eventually it dawned on me that whatever owned that face was very big and I had no idea where it was now. I went home to get my son but couldn't drag him out of the house that night.

From there, I dragged my son camping at the nearest site. I still didn't really believe what I had seen and the only recording equipment I could get my hands on was our little Digicam that only takes a short video and is slow to power up. This is not of any use when something may happen before the thing powers up. This, of course, was the night we got chattered at as well as hearing chimp noises and a pok-pok sound.

Forest Friends of the Night

About a week after my roadside encounter the family was all at my sister's and I was telling my father about what had been happening. We decided to go for a ride and check the roadside site. I'm not much of a tracker but Dad is. While I was checking the spot I saw the silhouette and Dad started walking toward where I'd seen something cross the road.

I found that the tree which was behind where the silhouette was located was actually rooted a few feet down the embankment. Behind it, at the base the ground was obviously well trampled. I looked but couldn't find any clear tracks. This discovery did illustrate why it appeared so short though. I realized at my size, standing there, I'd stand about the same height it did.

Dad yelled for me to come check out what he'd found. There was a trackway coming up the steep, grassy embankment right where the flash had crossed the road. There were deep gouges that pulled out all the grass and roots with a five foot step. This wasn't a quadruped and whatever it was very heavy. Across the road was an obvious wide slide down the opposite embankment where the grass was still packed down from something sliding down it. Dad swore it looked like a big butt print.

I wasn't dressed explore the woods and Dad had recently had knee replacement surgery. He started to head down the slope to look for tracks in the water at the bottom but I stopped him, unwilling to let him risk hurting himself. I promised to return the next day... I woke up to the heaviest downpour I'd seen in ages and spent the rest of the day pacing and grumbling. I now I keep a bag of plaster, bucket, spare hikers and socks, sweats, etc in the truck, just in case...

Our overnight research sites are two miles and three and a half miles from where I had this encounter and have recorded some really interesting but inconclusive things in all three locations.

Apologies for the novella, but it does feel good getting it out there.

11. The Children

With some of the things I began hearing from others and the continued activity I was having, I not only knew then that they were real, I now began to realize there were many more than I would have ever thought. Not only are they in the northwestern areas of the country, but they are all over North America.

In my career, my job entails root cause investigations and how to assimilate information. At this point in my investigations into bigfoot, I was beginning to recognize common traits in that information.

I have not heard many stories of aggression at all. As a matter of fact, most stories are exactly the opposite. I was slowly turning the long held perception that they are the monsters I have always heard about. Instead, they are highly intelligent Forest People with a complex social structure. I have heard of this from people like Arla Williams and Thom Cantrall who have had years' worth of interactions. I have excelled greatly in understanding of that.

There have been many wonderful moments that I have had. Many of these involved children... One such story happened one fall weekend in Georgia:

The Apples

During an early fall camp out in 2012 on our hunting property, Cathy and I had the opportunity to share our camp with a friend. We had brought our grandson Hunter Garrett who was seven at the time with us. Arla had taught us the bigfoot people liked to watch us and especially enjoyed watching children having fun. The goal was to just camp, have fun and see if the bigfoot people responded.

We had brought some apples with us as we thought it would be a great idea to "gift" them to the bigfoot. It didn't take me but a few seconds to "know" where these should go. There was an area the bigfoot people used to observe us that was close to our camp. This spot was approximately a hundred yards behind one of our campers and they had just made an arch a few days prior with a thirty foot tall pine tree.

Forest Friends of the Night

After pulling the pine down, they used an old dead tree that had fallen a couple of years that was located about ten feet away. They moved it and placed it on the top of the pine tree, thereby pinning it to the ground. There were several other breaks and bows leading up to our camp.

I took a bag with seven apples in it and Hunter and I rode my four wheeler to the area to place the apples out as our gift. Beside the bowed pine there was a tree break that was only about three feet high and the top of the tree was at just the proper angle to place the apples in a line on the tree. Hunter got five of the apples placed in a line with no problem but the sixth apple proved more difficult as it rolled off when placed by the others. He tried several times without success until I finally told him not to worry about putting it there.

I told him, "Place the last two apples on the tree stump there next to the pinned pine."

He then placed the last two on the stump and we drove the four wheeler back to camp and proceeded to just enjoy the evening.

We grilled out, talked and watched Hunter play. Nothing at all interesting happened though. There were just the sounds of us talking and Hunter playing. Later, as we sat up and talked, we did hear some interesting vocalizations but they were not very close to us.

The next day I awoke before the others. I rode the four wheeler over to the area we had left the apples and the first thing I noticed was that there was only one apple on the stump. I didn't think too much of it at that time because any woods critter could have taken the apple. Then I realized something very interesting... there were six apples on the leaned over tree! There were not the five Hunter had placed there, but six.

I was amazed... This meant the bigfoot people had to have done this. We had locked the gate to our camp and we were the only ones there. It also meant that they MUST have watched Hunter try to get the six apples on that tree. I immediately thought to myself, they were showing me proof in a very subtle but sure way, they were here and they were watching us.

I had made a short video of us placing the apples the day before and then again a video of me walking over to the area the next day and seeing the apples. I drove back into camp to find my wife was awake. I immediately showed her the video. We were both very happy with what they had shown us.

Forest Friends of the Night

The Conference

Alex (Midnight Walker), another friend I met through a Forum, hosted a Bigfoot Conference in Georgia in the winter of 2013. He had a list of speaker's that were wonderful and there were many people that came to stay for both Saturday and Sunday. One of those was an eleven year old boy. Here is his story:

Elijah's Story

There was a young boy about eleven years old in attendance with his mother. He was extremely interested in the subject, to say the least as he sat in the front row of the conference area listening to every word from every speaker. He was there for both days and accompanied me and a few others as we had a little night sit out in area of sightings at the home of our Dahlonega, Georgia area hosts.

This night was very interesting, to say the least, as we had researchers there as well. One brought a wooden flute and, as he played, the wooded hill beside us came alive with leaves rustling and obvious footsteps. Many there heard them and a while later there was eye shine from our visitors. Most of those present saw this.

We could hear them walking and see their movement on the hill. Elijah was so excited... He was talking to them as one person would talk to another. He had no fear and was absolutely amazed.

On the last day of the conference, the boy sat outside the conference center and he was very sad that it was ending. As he sat there, he told his mother that he knew they were there last night on the hill and he had asked them over and over to show him they were there so he would know for sure. (I will add here I didn't know this part until later.)

As we were leaving the conference area, going down the road we had driven several times a day up to and including this morning, the Inukshuk was seen by my wife on a bank beside the road. We stopped and took photos with another friend who was there.

That evening as we arrived home I was on Facebook posting pictures of the conference and I posted the picture of the Inukshuk. These were used by Native Americans and the traditional meaning of the Inukshuk is "Someone was here" or "You are on the right path." One of the responses I got on the photograph was from the boy's mother.

She told me the story of how he had asked the bigfoot people to show him they were there. The boy spotted this on his way home, squealing with delight to his mother "They made it for me!"

They had left him a stack of rocks to show him they were there! He had no idea of the meaning of the Inukshuk. At that point, I posted the story on Facebook and everyone that was there agreed that it was not there a few hours earlier.

I do know from my experience with many researchers, and even myself that the sasquatch people know much of the Native American's ways and traditions. I have, on many occasions, seen their signs, stick formations, etc. that offer evidence of this. Was it left for the boy by them? In his mind, it absolutely was. In my mind, maybe, but it really doesn't matter, the boy got his answer.

In relating children's stories, have heard them described as hairy people, hairy friends, hairy boys etc. The personal stories I have heard never call them monsters... Why is that? Most young people are very honest in their stories and interpretations. Maybe we could learn some valuable lessons listening to our children?

12. Forest Friends

As the year 2012 began to wind down and fall arrived, we made the now familiar trip down to the property again. This trip was different as I had a different view of the woods. Knowing the bigfoot people were there excited me and my thoughts of them being dangerous were completely gone. I looked into the dark woods before going to bed that Friday night... I smiled and said, "Goodnight friends" just as if they were right in front of me. I felt a joy and peace inside of me I had never enjoyed before. It was like a comfort knowing they were there, just watching. My forest friends of the night were now a part of my life and it began a new way for me to look at things.

As I awoke I had a very relaxed feeling and was anxious to go out and "play" in the forest. Yes, I was using the excuse of deer hunting but that was secondary to my real reason for being there. What I needed most was to breathe

Forest Friends of the Night

in the fresh air, to feel the slight breeze and stir the woods awake from the night before.

    The sun was about to make its appearance as a tinge of orange grew larger and larger on the horizon. It was outlined by trees on the ridge ahead of me. I heard the familiar sound of an owl with his "who cooks for you" call. This morning seemed magical to me and I felt more alive than anytime I had remembered. I drove my ATV to a ladder tree stand that offered a great view of a green field with the steady sound of a creek rushing by. I made my way up the ladder and the owls were chatting it up quite loudly on the creek beside me although I never saw them. I could also hear the leaves  rustling just inside the tree line that blocked my view of a large hill across the creek.

    I was thinking it was either deer or, possibly someone on our property as the property line was just over the hill. The noises continued for a few minutes, diminishing as they grew further away from me until, in a few minutes, they were gone.

Forest Friends of the Night

As the sun rose higher and it began to warm, my stomach began to let me know it was time for lunch. I climbed down and began the trek back then I decided to visit the creek before leaving to just see if there was any sign of deer crossing. There were a few tracks, but what caught my eye was a mud puddle at the edge of the creek. There was a single print, foot shaped, in the mud and it had filled with water. It was very loose mud and didn't display toes that I could see, but, oddly enough, there were no more prints in front or behind the track! I found that very strange.

How could anyone, person or bigfoot, not have any more prints leading to or away from this one? It was just one of many odd and unexplainable events that I would see in the next couple of years.

As I made my way back to camp I noticed more and more bowed trees, broken branches on hardwoods and things that were not here last week. Things such as big rocks

Forest Friends of the Night

in trails, sticks making "x"s, woven trees and other odd things.

As I arrived in camp, I noticed on the table beside the camper there was a jay feather laying. This, in and of itself was not unusual, except that it had a round pebble laying top of it. HOW did that happen?

I began to chuckle at some of the things I found. They were subtle things yet very deliberately done. Those things kept happening and still do!

As the day got longer and night approached, the chorus of owls began again but this time they were at camp. A few minutes later a long low pitched howl began and it rose to a very high pitched scream at the end. That was promptly followed by a loud series of pops that was similar to what I had heard on the other property. I later came to know these as tree knocks as was described in many stories. I had heard others describe these as something the bigfoot do... a bigfoot behavior. Later while lying in bed, we could hear little rocks landing on top of the camper! They were just small ones and it only happened every few minutes, but it was steady.

13. The Good, Bad and the Ugly

Things had been happening so very fast and many times I had to stop and pinch myself. Was this all a dream that I just could not wake from? After many pinches and many days, I decided pinching myself did not feel too good so, again, I immersed in Facebook and the  forums. I kept asking questions and being introduced to people as I was learning from them all I could. I quickly began to notice there were little groups of people inside the larger "Bigfoot Community". I call them the Good, Bad and the Ugly.

The Good were those that seemed so very knowledgeable. They had real answers that I could most relate too and they could explain things in a way that made complete sense to me. Many times these same people would help me simply by listening and accepting what I said without ridicule. These people I categorized as the "Good".

There was another group of people that seemed very knowledgeable but spent more time spouting their experience and how they were the ones in the know. They also got a lot of attention because they sought out the spotlight. They were in the media interviews and to me seemed to almost seek out the camera for self-aggrandizement. Some of these people clearly had knowledge, but some of them said things to shoot down with a matter-of-fact tone that seemed brash and unaccepting of other's views. I called this group "The Bad".

They were not called bad because they were bad people, but because I felt their views confused the community as a whole. People would latch onto their celebrity status and label them as "experts". Well, I never could and never have accepted the word expert when it comes to the bigfoot people. How could anyone? There is much yet to learn... So much that we cannot explain. Some of the people I trusted totally and had years of experience felt the same way, THERE ARE NO EXPERTS!

The "Ugly" were those that were all over the groups posting lies, causing dissension or hoaxing for attention. Many of these people would rise to a cult following and almost celebrity status. Some people would believe anything these ugly people said and jump in their corner to defend them. Many of the new or young people that joined groups to learn would get caught up in this. This caused damage to many and prevented others even discussing anything relating to it. They would also get media and of course as the media does most often, they would run with a story of a hoax and everyone in the community would be labeled a hoaxer.

Some of the "Good" on my list and a recommendation to learn more about are Ron Morehead of "Sierra Sounds" fame. Ron also is researching the elongated heads in Peru and other places. http://ronmorehead.com/. Check out his books and works online.

R. Scott Nelson

Scott Nelson is a retired U.S. Navy Crypto Linguist specialist with over thirty years of experience. He has spent many years researching the "language" aspect of the bigfoot and has done extensive work on the Sierra Sounds audios as well as other vocals.

Thomas "Thom" Cantrall who has more than fifty years of experience going back to his days as a Forester. He has several books out on the subject. Check out his website for more. http://www.ghostsofrubyridge.com/.

Arla Collett Williams

Arla Colett Williams, whose books "My Life With the Hairy People" and "Respecting the Water" can be found on Amazon and at http://www.ghostsofrub yridge.com/arla-2/mylifewiththehairype ople/.

Bob Gimlin

Alex (Midnight Walker) has some of the best audios of anyone I have ever heard. Also, his teachings of the bigfoot have been phenomenal.

95

Forest Friends of the Night

Bob Gimlin was with Roger Patterson on that day in 1967 when the Patterson Gimlin Film was made. That film inspired me greatly as well as helping me to understand more. Although I have not personally met Bob, (yet) the conversations with Thom Cantrall regarding him are the next best thing!

There are a few others and many friends I have met on Facebook and conferences that have helped me greatly and I continue to share with them as we learn together.

My advice to any new people in this is to listen to opinions, but do plenty of research yourself prior to accepting anything as total truth. Listen with an open mind, but confirm as much as you can. Don't fall for the bad and be very careful of the "ugly."

14. The Interviews

One of the forums I participate in is the "Bigfoot Forums." I helped there as a moderator for a while and when I became too busy to participate much, I was asked to do the blog for that forum. I had an idea for the blog to use it to allow the members to ask written questions to some of the Bigfoot Community Members that had experience and were rather well known. Of course I gravitated to some of the people I thought would bring a lot of valuable information. I am including the following interviews of a few of the people I mentioned in the last chapter.

Ron Morehead and Scott Nelson

The Sierra Sounds are a series of vocalizations recorded from a remote hunting camp in the Sierra Nevada Mountains. A group of deer hunters, including Ron Morehead, recorded some of these sounds in 1971/72. Ron brought in Al Berry to help him understand what was happening. Al later captured more in the same remote location.

These vocalizations are extraordinary and are also the catalyst that later involved **Scott Nelson**, a twenty year Navy veteran with an added ten years of civilian experience who was skilled and highly trained in linguistics, specializing for many years in breaking codes and studying different languages. A quick explanation of the work done by a cryptolinguist is in order here.

As a cryptolinguist, Scott spent many, many hours listening to foreign radio transmissions... even in languages he did not speak. He spoke, of course, English, Spanish, Farsi (Iranian) and Russian. When a transmission was received in, say, Chinese, he had to be able to listen to it and determine if it was language or just gibberish transmitted to take up time and confuse anyone listening. He had to be able to tell, by flow of syllables if it was real language. If he so determined, it was then sent on to someone who could understand Chinese.

Scott brought that professional experience to do the most extensive research yet of the many vocals of reported Sasquatch. It all started for Scott the day his twelve year old son was doing a report for school on Sasquatch/Bigfoot and he heard Ron's tapes on the internet.

Forest Friends of the Night

Here are those 2 interviews:

Ron Morehead

Interviewer - Did you see any of the subjects making the sounds?

Ron - Yes, however, you're probably referencing the sounds Al Berry taped, which seemed very close to the mic. His microphone was remotely placed about forty feet up from our shelter. We think the creature was behind one of the huge trees there. Each time he would stick his head out of an opening, made earlier in the roof, the sounds would stop. On that night, he saw nothing...nobody did.

Interviewer: I ask because the recorder must have been made very close to the subject in order to get such a clear result.

Interviewer - Mr. Morehead, did you ever feel threatened or feel fear during these encounters?

Ron - Because of the unknown, it's difficult to not feel a bit insecure; however, after we didn't shoot our guns and they didn't come crashing through the shelters' walls, we became less fearful.

That's when we began to look forward to the night-time and their visits.

Interviewer - I know he believes that Patty is a real bigfoot. Is there any other footage that he considers to be the real deal, based on what he has seen/heard?

Ron - I don't consider myself a film analyzer…some very well could be, but I usually let others accredit or dismiss. I don't like to get involved in something when I don't know the context of the situation or the people involved.

Interviewer - Do you find it frustrating in the years that have passed since the recordings that the research community has made little to no impact on the scientific acceptance of the animal you recorded?

Ron - Understanding the constraints that science works within, and how they need to stay inside that boundary of proof, I don't have a problem with it. They must assume it's just another wild unidentified animal running around in the woods until evidence can show them something different.

Interviewer - Have you ever been approached by any type of Government authority regarding what you recorded?

Ron - NO

Interviewer - Do you have any idea, even if not confirmed, of how many animals there were present at the time of the recording and how/what did you personally feel their persona and/or intentions were ?

Ron - Usually we could estimate how many there were by the direction of the sounds and the interaction they were having with each other. At first we thought the aggression must have been directed at us, but in retrospect, I think they were squabbling among themselves, probably over the food left out.

Interviewer - How were the recordings obtained?

Ron - Cassette Recorders, night-time conditions.

Interviewer - Circumstances surrounding the actual recording of these creatures?

Ron - During the first couple years they would only come around after we went into the shelter and closed the opening. It wasn't until 1974 that they became interactive with us while we were outside the shelter. The details of these events are more thoroughly covered in the CDs and my book.

Interviewer - How close were the Bigfoot from the recorder?

Ron - They were not that close to the recorders, but often close to the remote microphones. I don't know how far from the mics they may have been — different times, different distances, but often seemingly very close. Great Apes have a way of making their sounds travel with a lot of amplitude by squeezing their air sacks with their upper arms. This could be one of their attributes.

Interviewer - I'm sure someone has to have tried this, has playing back the recordings out in the field consistently drawn physical responses and /or vocal replies that were similar or the same?

Ron - No, actually never. We tried it a couple times at camp, but it didn't work. Then we thought, "What if what we previously recorded was not nice?"…we had no idea what they were saying. I don't encourage folks do this with these sounds.

Interviewer - There are hundreds of questions I could ask. This took place at a remote deer camp that I assume he owned and or had access to. Was this a one season thing or was there ongoing interaction/observations (I considered listening an observation of your surroundings), and if it was not how many years did he observe activity in the area?

Ron - The hunting camp is located on Federal land, about an 8-mile trek on an imposing trail in the Sierra Mountains. The events were on-going, and the close-up sounds stopped in 1976 (began in 1971). Since then, we've had occasional glimpses, a couple good sightings, but mostly the sounds are from a distance now. The most recent event for me was in 2012 when I heard chatter from a distance, then a 'bang' on one of our barrels, and heard bi-pedal walking around the stove area.

Interviewer - Mr. Morehead, have you ever had any other experiences with what he may think was a Sasquatch in other areas he has been?

Ron - Yes, I've had other incidents in other areas, but never like the ones at our Sierra camp.

Interviewer - Mr. Morehead, Have you or Scott Nelson gotten together and compared notes or taken new recordings from other researchers with valid sound captures and given feedback and/or springboard what they may learn from them to extend their own research?

Ron - Scott and I have been to the Sierra camp together, but he's never been able to capture more corroborative sounds. Scott often gets inundated with folks sending him sounds of yells, grunts, or moans, but so far he has not received any sounds that have a morpheme stream (several words that make up a sentence) which would allow him to state that the source had language. He uses our Sierra recordings as a comparison.

Interviewer - This is a follow up question in regard to possible government involvement - Have the recordings been analyzed or otherwise commented upon by anyone from a government research agency, such as Yerkes, Oregon, or the California National Primate Research Centers? If so, what were their comments/opinions? If not, why?

Ron - *Government agencies do not take this subject seriously… at least not publicly. Over the years we tried many times to obtain help from qualified institutions. Most, however, put us in the looney-tunes box and wouldn't respond seriously. We actually paid a few to try and give us an unbiased report. One told us they thought they heard words being spoken and therefore discredited the recordings (but kept the money). Another told Al Berry that the original recorder he sent to them was not the recorder that recorded the sounds…that was just wrong, but kept they money. Another told me that they'd tell us what made the sounds in three days, guaranteed. They wanted five thousand dollars up front…didn't fall for that one. The stories go on and on regarding our efforts. Dr. Kirlin's report gave credibility to the recordings but it was semi-quantitative. Scott Nelson's statement clarified the language issue, and it seems more and more folks are now reporting that they are hearing these creatures' chatter (similar to Albert Ostman's account of 1924).*

Larry Johnson (one of the hunters) had a fairly good sighting from just a few feet away on a moonlit night, from a small hole within the shelter's wall. He claimed it was over eight feet tall, broad shoulders, and no neck. Most of the sightings have been brief...never has one of these creatures been caught napping. My daughter (Rhonda) has had very good sightings. She described one as being about eight foot tall, thin but with broad shoulders, and turned with its head and body together—no neck. The one I got a glimpse of was the night I recorded them while Bill McDowell and I were by our stove. It was moving so fast I could not make out any details.

Interviewer - Is there any reason he has not been able to subsequently record sounds of the same quality since the original recordings?

Ron - Although I usually take a recorder with me, sometimes I don't. It's not important for me to obtain more vocalizations. My goal is to understand them better, and it seems they are very tuned-in to exploitation. Although they have humanistic attributes, they seem to be able to stealthily out maneuver us. They are not altogether human. I believe they are a hybrid with attributes we don't understand yet.

Interviewer - If anyone is interested in reading a more detailed account of the Sierra Sounds incidents, you should get a copy of *Bigfoot* by Alan Berry and B. Ann Slate. The first third of the book relates the circumstances surrounding the recordings. Also, "Voices in the Wilderness," is my book which I recently released that includes a CD sound track.

My questions for Mr. Morehead are:

1.   How closely does the above-mentioned book relate the facts of the incidents as he knows them? It's good and tells the story from Al Berry's perspective. Al was diligently looking to uncover a hoax... he never could.

2.   **Does Mr. Morehead consider bigfoot to be just another animal like bear, deer, apes, and even humans, or does he believe there is something "more" to them?**

Ron - I believe there is much more to them, and suggest reading my articles at www.bigfootsounds.com

Interviewer - Regarding the 911 call you discuss on your blog from the early 1990's, what more can you tell us about that and what did you learn?

Ron - If a dog irritates, or begins to chase one of these creatures, it will probably not return...at least not alive. This man's German Shepard was tossed thirty five feet, over a fence after it was 'thumped' on the ground (probably dead then). My suggestion is

to not take dogs on expeditions. I don't think these creatures really want to kill your dog, but they will if irritated.

Scott Nelson

Hi Scott... and thank you very much for agreeing to answer questions from our forum members. These will be submitted in our blog as an ongoing learning process to help understand what research is being done from some of the most notable researchers in the BF Community. We appreciate your time to help us learn more about the sasquatch people.

Interviewer - Have you contacted any Phoneticists in regard to the various recordings you now have?

Reason for asking... With the perception of language in the recordings and that it was done with a human-like vocal system, the phonemes containing quantal vowels can be studied, measured and quantified using the relationships of F1 and F2 formats. With the three quantal vowels or cardinal vowels being attributed to humans only among mammals according to Anthropologists, this would be quite telling.

Scott - *You are quite right about this and I am sure that someday these studies will be done on Sasquatch Language, just as they have been done on Human Language. Phoneticists and those specializing in Linguistics are the very scientists that Ron spoke of in his interview, and as of yet, they want nothing to do with these sounds. I have offered to present my study to some of the most eminent Linguistics Specialists in the world, but have been rejected every time due to concerns for their academic reputations. One gentleman in England wanted us to box everything up and send it to him, but with a little research I discovered that he was a professional skeptic with a definite agenda. I have always been willing to present the study to anyone who will listen, and of course we are always looking for others who are willing to take the same academic risks that we have.*

Interviewer - Mr Nelson, Could you please explain in layman terms why you think language exists in the recordings you've heard?

Scott - *It might be best to start here with my arguments for the three conclusions that I drew almost immediately upon hearing the Sierra Sounds for the first time. Probably the best way to do that is to copy some of the notes I use when I present my study at conferences and symposiums: After that first quick review of the samplings of the Sierra Sounds, there were three facts that were immediately evident to me: (1) The vocalizations are not human (as we currently define human) (2) The creatures were speaking in a complex language (by the human definition of language) and (3) The tapes could not have been faked.*

Forest Friends of the Night

First: The voices are not human. The creatures on the Berry/Morehead Tapes are producing sounds that humans cannot make. Their vocal range is far too great; much lower and much higher than humans are capable of producing. This fact is corroborated by the Kirlin study. Additionally, the volume and resonance of many of the vocalizations they produce is far beyond the ability of humans. However, the most striking element to note is the prosody of utterance, or the tempo at which each utterance is delivered, as well as the speed at which the conversational turns take place, with the creatures almost stepping on each other in their discourse. For the majority of the utterances, the rate of deliverance is at least twice that of humans.

My second conclusion: It is a complex, human-like language. What did I recognize in the vocalizations that told me that it was language? First are the articulated phonemes (individual units of phonetic sound) so similar to our own that it must be assumed they are produced by the same apparatus that we possess, namely, the tongue, the teeth and the lips, along with the entire tracheal tree, oral cavity and nasal cavity. I have isolated thirty nine different phonemes, all common to human language. Phonemes combine to form morphemes, or individual units of meaning which we commonly call syllables or minimal words. These are evident throughout the tapes, repeated in conversational turns and morpheme streams characteristic only of language. We

*find discourse (conversational turns of utterance), query inflection
and direct response, imperative or persuasive inflections,
expression of emotion, intimidation, negation and even ritual.
These vocalizations exhibit characteristics that are conventional,
automatized, arbitrary and creative; all of which are properties of
human language.*

*In brief, there are so many characteristics of human
language evident in the tapes that we must assume that even those
elements that cannot yet be known, such as grammatical
categories, are also present in this language.*

*Finally to my third conclusion: The tapes could not have been
faked. While serving as a crypto-linguist working with Naval
Intelligence, I trained in every form of deceptive voice
communication imaginable, including slowing the tape; speeding it
up; modulation of tone and pitch; playing tape backward and
distortion of every kind. None of these techniques is evident here.
I was a Russian analyst so I trained in all of the Soviet tactics of
deception. They are the best in the world at deceptive
communication techniques, but even their best effort could not
have produced these vocalizations; and certainly, no one could have
done it in 1974. What initially led me to conclude that the tapes
were not fake, is that in numerous instances the humans and the
creatures are speaking at the same time; vocally stepping on each*

other. *This cannot be done without leaving trace evidence (also confirmed by the Kirlin Study).*

At this juncture, to claim that these vocalizations were faked, one would have to argue that a secret cabal, comprised of several ingenious conspirators, was so determined to deceive the world, that they invented their own language, modulated their vocalizations to frequencies above and below the ability of humans, harassed a small group of well-armed hunters, over a period of several weeks in successive years and threw in numerous cognate words and expressions to boot. It is now more reasonable to defend the existence of an undocumented creature than it is to believe in such a conspiracy.

Interviewer - If there is a language involved does it sound similar to any known languages and if so which one?

Scott - When I first stumbled onto the Sierra Sounds, labeled "Samurai Chatter" on a website, they did indeed sound Asian due to the rapidly staccato nature and deep throated delivery. I immediately took the sounds to a Native-Japanese colleague of mine who said, "It sounds like an ancient form of Japanese, but I can't understand a single word." I have since played the tapes to native speakers of virtually every human language group, to include Russian, Spanish, Persian, and several Native-American, African and Pacific Island Languages. All of these native speakers have heard "words" that are familiar to them. This has led me to conclude that it is natural for us to listen for morpheme streams that have meaning for us; however, we cannot conclude that these are cognatic words and phrases from human languages.

If Sasquatch is as intelligent and observant as we think he is, it would also be natural for him to assimilate parts of our language. If his very survival depends on avoidance of humans, would he not want to know what we are thinking and planning? He certainly would and for the same reasons that I did what I did in the Navy, "Know Thine Enemy,"

If Sasquatch followed us to the New World over the Bearing Straits, he would likely carry remnants of Asiatic languages. His language would have evolved along the periphery of Native-American culture. Spanish has been a dominant language on this continent for more than five hundred years and English for more than four hundred. Therefore, I believe that Sasquatch could be using elements from all of these influences, as well as his own language system that would be very different from known languages.

Interviewer - Mr. Nelson, Why did you ever decide to make a separate Sasquatch Phonetic Alphabet, when all of the sounds can be phonetically transcribed using the current International Phonetic Alphabet (IPA). The IPA contains all sounds that can be made with a vocal tract. Why did you feel it necessary to make a new alphabet?

Scott - *The IPA is extremely complicated for any non-specialist to understand, using many symbols that look nothing like "letters" in any common language and which for most researchers (including myself) are impossible to find on any keyboard, let alone pronounce. Without specialized training in Linguistics, the IPA would be useless. Therefore, the quick answer is: I decided to create a phonetic alphabet that is more accessible to a broad spectrum of researchers; knowing that the real evidence for Sasquatch Language would not come from academics who have never stepped foot in the woods, but from the front-line dedicated lay-persons who invest virtually everything they have to spend week after week out there amongst these beings.*

I utilized variations of modern English Reformed Phonetic Alphabets as well as elements of the International NATO Transliteration Alphabet with which all military Crypto-Linguists are familiar. This makes for a much more research-friendly tool, very useful for those of us who are doing the hard work. We will let the academics do what they do when we are finished.

Interviewer - Mr. Nelson, What were the key things you noticed about the Sierra Sounds speech that clued you in that it was possibly language? Do you think that the Sasquatch "language" can/will eventually be translated into an existing human language? Is there a possibility that the sounds (language) were produced by a human?

Scott - There is no possibility that the sounds were produced by a human. Please see my answer to number 2 for my argument as well as what is it that makes this language.

"Translation" can never truly take place until meaning can be confirmed by the speaker, so that is something that will not be happening anytime soon.

Interviewer - Mr. Nelson, Are there examples of other audio recordings that have demonstrated the same language characteristics that you have identified in the Sierra recordings?

Scott - I have just a couple of short clips that fit this description, but nothing of the clarity and extent of the Sierra recordings. That, of course, is our Holy Grail.

Interviewer - Mr. Nelson, you have concluded that a distinct language was detected. As an expert in your field, do you think the communications are of a hostile nature, or maybe an effort on the sasquatch's part to communicate with humans?

Scott - If we presume that Sasquatch possesses similar emotional sensibilities as humans and would express them in a similar fashion, then indeed we find emotional utterances throughout the Berry/Morehead recordings. We can infer much of this from modulations in pitch, tone and degree of agitation in the voice, and from the meaning of presumed cognatic expressions. Since emotion is so often swayed by external environmental stimuli, it is easy to understand why the range of emotions expressed by the creatures during this confrontation between species, would be quite narrow: apprehension, aggravation, and hostility are most common. However, there are many instances where curiosity, wonder and even humor are expressed; most notably at BI-1:30.19 (Berry Tape) where I posit that the male creature is laughing.

We are quite sure that on the Morehead Tape, the creatures are attempting to slow down their utterances in order to communicate with the humans.

Interviewer - Mr. Nelson, have you analyzed any audio recordings where the bigfoot speaks a known human language that seems authentic? I would imagine there are a lot of hoaxes out there. If a recording seems authentic and not human in origin, is there any way to determine from the recording if the speaker is communicating in a human language known to it or if it is just mimicry?

Scott - I have received many audio clips that certainly are attempts to deceive, others that are just misidentified animal sounds and still others that simply cannot be determined to be outside of human ability to produce. The rest of your question I believe I answered in (2) and (3) above.

Interviewer – Mr. Nelson, can you please clarify that when you use the word " language ", you are not describing languages of the human species which are divided geographically such as English, Spanish, Mandarin etc but

are describing the word as a form of communication like many animals are supposed to have, like Orca's for example? Or, are you saying that this "language " is more similar on a technical level to actual human languages than what other forms of communication in the animal world is said to be ?

Scott - *What is evident on the Berry/Morehead Tapes is language by the human definition of it. Virtually all of the phonemes recovered are common to human languages, therefore, we have to assume they are articulated with the same apparatus humans have. Please see above where I expand on this.*

Interviewer - Is there a correlation between the speed of a spoken language and intelligence of the speaker and if so what does that say about the bigfoot's IQ?

Scott - *I am not qualified to judge on this issue. Humans speak in such a wide range of delivery rates and certainly, we speak quickly when we are in a heightened state of excitement. I do not believe that all humans who speak rapidly are more intelligent than those who speak more slowly. In fact, I have found that highly intelligent people tend to slow their delivery, giving some thought to what they are going to say and wanting to insure comprehension by the listener. I believe, however, that sasquatch is a highly intelligent and even sentient being, since it is by our* *having the ability for Language that we define ourselves as sentient beings.*

Interviewer – Mr. Nelson, when you first heard the Sierra Sounds as your son was doing his research project on bigfoot, what was the first thing you thought when you heard it? Did you think it was a potential hoax? Also, when was the WOW moment that you knew they were real?

Scott - The "WOW" moment was immediate and there was no possibility that it was a hoax.

Interviewer - What kind of advice on equipment can you give researchers that want to do their own recordings?

Scott - I am certainly no sound equipment expert. Ron and I have had good service from the ZOOM H2 voice recorder.

Interviewer - When people do "call blasting" using recordings like the Sierra Sounds or others, is there a potential danger of what they are telling the other bigfoot? Is there a chance the sounds could be "not so nice" and would create a potential bad encounter?

Forest Friends of the Night

Scott - There is always the chance that some of the utterances on the Bery/Morehead Tapes are not so nice. I have always thought that call-blasting was rather silly and ineffective. I am quite convinced that they are much smarter than we ever wanted to believe and that they cannot be fooled for long by call blasting. In fact, I think it drives them away. I think it is much more effective to just go out into the woods, do the things that we silly humans normally do, be nonthreatening and thereby invite their curiosity.

On 4/17/2014 Thom Cantrall conducted an interview with Mr. Bob Gimlin over lunch near his Yakima, WA home. The questions for this interview came from members of the Bigfoot Forum as the result of a call for "what would you ask Bob?" type of scenario. Here is that interview in full including all vocal pauses, stutters and fits and starts as recorded on that day. The original video of that interview is in the possession of Mr. Cantrall, and will remain so. The names used by the questioners or the names used on that Forum.

Bob Gimlin

The Interview:

Bob Gimlin Interview
4/7/2014
by Thom Cantrall

The questions asked in this interview came mainly from one of the author's forum groups and were forwarded to Thom Cantrall, who then conducted the interview with Mr. Gimlin on the seventh of April, 2014.

Thom: Did you think film would solve the mystery and gain public acceptance? ... when you first made the film...

Bob: I definitely did not think it'd solve the problem... it did not even solve the problem with me.

Thom: Do you regret not shooting Patty which would have assured recognition almost fifty years ago?

Bob: No I don't... I had no intentions to unless I thought that I HAD to.

Thom: During the encounter, did you feel concern for your or your colleagues or horse's safety?

Bob: Yes, I did somewhat. I didn't know how much or what to expect.

Thom: Do you feel you have retreated or shot the creature if it had turned and threatened you?

Bob: Yes, I do... I've always said I feel I would have shot and I wasn't sure with something that size. At that time I was an excellent shot. And I had one hundred eighty grain... 30'06 one hundred eighty grain and I'd shot a lot of elk with that same projectile.

Thom: Did you see observe the tracks immediately after seeing the Bigfoot?

Bob: Yes, I did.

Thom: Were the ground conditions suitable for leaving tracks like that and do you remember thinking something wasn't quite right with them?

Bob: the tracks were...

Thom: I'm not sure what that means...

Bob: I don't either what that means. The tracks were well acceptable for tracks for what that type of soil was.

Thom: Have you had any other eye witness events since then... have you had any close non-visual encounters?

Bob: Yes, I have.

Thom: Yes, one was on that trip... (The trip Bob took on the Pacific Crest Trail when he rode from Mexico to Canada the full length of the Pacific Crest Trail)

Bob: One was on that trip... one was up at Bumping... (Bumping Lake in the Cascade Mountains, just east of Mt. Rainier in Washington)

Thom: When was that?

Bob: Around 6 years ago.

Thom: Are there currently any active Bigfoot field/academic investigators that, in your opinion, are on the cutting edge of research or worthy of exceptional credibility?

Bob: I think that's a definite yes on that.

Thom: Could you explain why you feel this way about them?

Bob: OK, I feel this way particularly because I know the people individually and they are doing the very, very best they can in the field research at this time. There's been some, uh, uh, tremendous things happen in my opinion.

Forest Friends of the Night

Thom: Bob, the old saying that hindsight is 20:20 is there anything you wish you had done differently then, from the beginning of your search to the end result of having the footage?

Bob: Well, that's changed over the years... Yes, there's a lot of things I would have done differently the first thirty five years. The first thing was, I wouldn't have been down there to start with!

Thom: Chuckle... Yeah, I hear that!

Thom: Are there any videos that you have seen that you think are real?

Bob: I haven't really witnessed very many videos so the ones I have seen I leave an open book there of, it looks pretty good but, uh... and I'm not going to say, "not quite good enough," but there's always that question now...

Thom: What would you consider the area most likely to encounter a bigfoot these days?

Bob: Well, I've always said the Olympic Peninsula (of Washington) in my opinion is a great area. But, you're limited there for foliage and also for rain so I, uh, have changed my mind somewhat over the years. I used to say over the years I think the Olympic Peninsula is your best shot. Well, I strongly believe that now, maybe back down in the Willow Creek area and that partic...

that radius within a hundred miles or fifty is probably as good a place as any because of the way everything lies there... the mountain range and that close to the ocean and also the rivers and uh, the privacy.

Thom: Just to add... of the places I've been that I've found, that southeastern Oklahoma area is absolutely alive with them.

Bob: See, that's it, I've never been east to some of those places that I hear about so I don't really know. I've been to the Olympic Peninsula, I've been to Bumping Lake and I've been in California and those have always been... uh... we've heard sounds... and somewhat... of course, the film footage itself speaks for the California area. uh.. So that's my opinion as far as that part of it goes.

Thom: Did seeing Patty change anything about how you see the world?

Bob: Oh, definitely. 'Cause I never... I was a ... Basically I'm telling the truth, I was a skeptic up til that time... That they must exist but I was kinda like old Harry Truman, I had to see to totally believe. (interruption) Anyway, at that particular time the only thing I was going by was what Roger had talked to me about and played those cassette tapes (Roger used to play cassettes of people's testimonies about sightings when he and Bob were camped on their trail rides) *that other... the testimonials of other people. I thought Yes... they are probably there... there must be something there but I wanna see it!*

Thom: Did you hear Patty make any vocalizations of any kind? By this I mean, I don't necessarily mean screams or yells, but.. uh, grumbling noises or any type of sound... did she make any kind of noise or sounds?

Bob: If she did, I never heard it... there were so many things were happening so quickly... uh, and the horses moving... Roger moving... me trying to get settled in to help him in case I had to...

Thom: It's like the case of the old adage, when you're up to your tail in alligators, it's hard to remember your initial objective was to drain the swamp...

Bob: Chuckle... That's right... Exactly Thom... that is exactly it

Thom: You have been following the work of Bill Munns, what is your opinion on that?

Bob: uh.. Well I.. When I met Bill Munns and found out what he was doing... I met him and was really impressed... and for what he's doing at this present time... I don't know exactly... I will know this weekend but I take my hat off to Bill Munns for what he's done actually for my credibility part of it and so, to me, Bill Munns is really high on my list. Very very high on my list.

Thom: I'll echo that... very high on mine too... He has done fantastic work...

Bob: He has indeed.

Thom: Have you seen any other bigfoot photos that look like what you saw?

Bob: Well, some have come about as, uh, close as I that I could still identify that and I, uh, really, uh, most of the ones I see show a face and, uh, and the body part of it, uh, will deviate a little and I understand that there is going to be differences in body of bigfoot, so therefore, I say whatever they saw and took a picture of or described is probably as accurate as my description of … of … of Patty, and... but I did she her face very clearly and some of those are very, very close.

Thom: Have you seen anyone at any time, able to duplicate exactly what you saw that day in 1967?

Bob: No, I haven't seen anyone that totally duplicated it because with... when Patty walked away with that tremendous amount of muscle underneath that hair moving, uh, it's pretty hard to duplicate that, uh, in a picture or anything else in my opinion.

Thom: You're right, that was...

Thom: Besides the adrenaline rush and fear factor operating... uh... besides the adrenaline rush and fear factor operating, did you still get the hair on the back of your neck rising that day?

Bob: Well, I definitely did, yes, I, uh, uh, I finally realized these creatures do exist and here's one right in front of me... walking away from me with a size and muscle that I never dreampt that any creature could ever have..

Thom: We covered that... (We had covered the question of the number of sightings he's had... three.. Patty, the one on the Pacific Crest Trail and one at Bumping Lake)

Thom: What was the closest you got to Patty?

Bob: Well, es.. this is an estimated distance... the closest I got was when I first saw her and I'd say that was probably sixty feet... uh.. just a ball park figure was sixty feet or less.

Thom: have you ever had any doubts that Patty was anything other than 100% real?

Bob: Never have... Uh, with all the litigation that's come out about that... with the different people saying they were in a suit down there... I knew in my own mind and watching that and being right there that if couldn't have been a man in a suit.

Thom: If you could change one thing about that day in Bluff Creek, what would that be?

Bob: That people earlier on the film footage would have accepted it... what's been proven in the past and left me and my wife alone for the first thirty five years.

Thom: Do you think there is any possibility that there is a question about that day at Bluff Creek that you have not been asked... chuckle

Bob: Not really. It seems like I have been asked so many different questions. ... I meant... I think possibly that I have forgotten some of... some of the most basic events because of my age and because of the injuries I have sustained over the years

Thom: There are sources that you an... that you had Bob Heronimous's horse na... uh, named Chico at Bluff Creek.

Bob: Okay... I did have Bob Heronimous's horse because Roger had, apparently, borrowed that horse from Bob Heronimous. 'Cause I never got the horses together to go. Roger gathered up the horses... I had the transportation and I knew the horse. I'd been around the horse before... Big, stout... good roping horse and I think Bob used him back in those days to rope on but Bob Heronimous actually had that horse early in some of the work he was doing for Roger as well as myself where Roger was trying to get together a film to generate revenue to go on an expedition.

Thom: Did you ever consider the possibility that Patty was trying to lead you away from her young?

Bob: Well, I never had enough time to even think about that. I just knew she was walking away... didn't even know that they suspected a young or other one in because at that particular time, I knew about the three different sizes of tracks we'd been called down there for but I hadn't... I wasn't ... I was tired from the long distances we'd been riding at the time we'd been down there... so I never gave it any thought about her trying to lead me away from anything...

Thom: yeah...

Thom: The film is considered to be the gold standard of bigfoot evi.. evidence. Is there any other video, photo, et cetera that you find impressive?

Bob: No.

Thom: And what would you say to the people that think it's a hoax?

Bob: I say you ought to take a good look at the film footage and realize that there is gonna possibly be people out there try to make a story out of this. Forever that they're gonna say they were in a suit in northern California when Roger and I were there... and it's been done more than one time as far as I know... in fact, I didn't even realize that Greg Long had had somebody... a big guy, uh, six or seven years before he got ahold of Bob Hermonimous and tried to prove he was in a suit down there. So, You know, it kinda is a... a two sword, double sword or double edged question for me because I don't really know... the thing is... is... I just know that's what happened and I'm going by what happened.

Thom: Right

Thom: Upon seeing... this is a good question... Upon seeing Patty, what was your first thought? What were you feeling?

Bob: There's a great big thing and they really do exist.

Thom Chuckle... yeah... that is the first thought, isn't it?

Bob: that's the first thought I thought of...

Thom: The first... first time I saw one here to there and yeah... standing there looking at him and said "where are the experts now?..."

Bob: Exactly, Yeah... Well, I thought "All doubt is gone..."

Forest Friends of the Night

Thom: You've already said it is not an ape you saw in 1967... Could you have guessed what it was?

Bob: No... uh.. you know I, I.. could not... all I knew was it was a big, hairy covered human like creature walking away with a... with a great stride and a great, uh, amount of muscle mass and so, that's the only thing I could come up with. I had no idea...

Thom: It's mind boggling, isn't it?

Bob: Yes it was... definitely was...Still is to my...

Thom: Right...

Bob: after all the evidence... all the sightings that people have had, and all of the... all of everything that has happened since 1967 that's given me more strength about that than uh, than prior.

Thom: Do you have any idea why your forty seven year old piece of evidence is still the most convincing that they do exist? Like, why hasn't something been found to better prove it?

Bob: Well, yes, there's questions in my mind about that, but, you know, there's no way to really address them, 'cause in my opinion, uh, there's been a lot of effort to... to get more evidence. The only other thing I could come up with.. I have no proof... their ability to stay away, uh, from the camcorders, whatever, and basically I can figure out a little bit of my own personal opinions why they avoid human beings so much now... especially modern human beings... whereas we've heard the native Americans had close contact with them as if they were just part of the, uh, they wouldn't bother, uh... they were there, they belonged to Mother Earth... And we start shooting at them or we start to gather evidence they really exist and they're just trying to live their own life and be left alone.

Thom: And, well, look... look at our society... who's want to be a part of that if they had a choice?

Bob: Well, I can't... I'd like to be the first one to the moon if I could to get away from all this.

Thom: Chuckle...

Thom: I know you told me in the past that her tracks went across the entire sandbar. My question is do you recall roughly how many were good, clear tracks... were there twelve to twenty... twenty to forty...

Bob: Good tracks?

Thom: Yeah...

Bob: Oh, I'd say roughly, fifty to sixty...

Thom: Fifty to sixty?

Bob: or maybe even more than that. I covered as many as I could with all the material I covered as many as I could with all the material I could gather off the dead tree. There was a pretty good line of tracks there... uh... Matter of fact is, I can't recall just how long that, uh, type of soil was there but I'd say probably, uh, a hundred yards almost... at least a hundred and fifty feet of that same type of soil (silted in) that had gathered up underneath that logjam or behind that logjam.

Thom: Uh huh... before it got into the rocky stretch?

Bob: Before it got into the gravel. ... You know, and my error was then, I wished Roger and I would have measured that... but, you know, you just don't think of all that...

Thom: and then you have the film to take care of...

Bob: Exactly. Plus, you've got a lot of other issues and October 20th the day's a little short already... and you're dealing with darkness early.

Thom: That's right... and none of us are professionals...

Bob: I was the furtherest thing from a professional and... and.. and apparently Roger was too... We did what we thought was the best thing at the time.

Thom: There have been claims that there were other bigfoot type animals at the sighting location. Did you ever see any others in addition to the one you filmed?

Bob: No I did not.

Thom: Ok, How many days were you and Roger at Bluff Creek? ... about twenty one days wasn't it?

Bob: Yeah... My estimation was about twenty one days down there. I never could decide whether it was the last day or so in September or the first of October because we'd been down there approximately three weeks.

Thom: Right

Thom: I'd like to ask if you recall any additional little things that Roger said to him that (you) haven't previously mentioned on the night of the filming and on the following day on their way back home... uh, you know.. personal type of things... what were his feelings?

Bob: Well... okay... the next day on the way home, uh, ok.. that has to be explained because there was no "next day". That next day was trying to get out of that area with a storm in there... and then, all night I drove and Roger slept most of the time while I did the driving. So... the only thing that was talked about that night after we got back to the truck is that, uh, what... what really happened that day and what he saw through the camera and what I felt I saw and smelled. So, Therefore, each thing that we talked about varied just a little and then, of course we went on to sleep... the next morning it was raining and, uh, things just kind of broke loose from there.

Thom: Was there an odor associated with her?

Bob: a what now?

Thom: Was there an odor? Did you smell her?

Bob: Yeah, yes, there was an odor... I thought it had kind of a... a skunky, mest... musty, skunky type of smell... Pretty stinky but with a must to it.

Thom: That's cool... Uhm...I think I have a couple I wrote that I wanted to ask too...

Thom: If you were to have that happen today, what would you do?

Bob: If that happened to me today, I would not ride across the creek with the horse... I would try my best to act real submissive and get as close to her as I possibly could instead of all the scramble that went on that day. Because if... if that happened to me again, I would hope that Roger didn't have a camera and was running after her to take a picture and I could try my best to get as close as I could and act submissive like... I want to be a friend... That's what I'd like to do and that's what I'd like to do today if I ever get another opportunity to get close to one again.

Thom: Do you have any regrets about the publishing of the film to the world?

Bob: Oh yes, I do... so many different issues on that it would take me days to go through all of it

15. The Friendly Welcome

The spring of 2013 rolled in with a new anticipation of not just what I was learning from others, but to learn from the bigfoot people themselves. I was still waiting for the really good visual face to face. My wife had experienced it and living it through her eyes was amazing. With all of the people I had met in person as well as those on the forums, it was an amazing time in my life. I was learning and seeing things happen now that gave me a voracious appetite for more of the same. The trip to our hunting camp now was a time of full anticipation... not of the hunt for game, but the interaction with the bigfoot people I now knew were very real.

We spent time in our hunting area and several things happened to let us know they were around. There were taps on the camper, an occasional rock being tossed on top of it and every night when we were there alone, we could hear noises in the night. As the next few months passed, things became even more exciting as Arla told me she was coming to Georgia this year. I had the opportunity to meet her, Thom, Ron Morehead, Scott Nelson and many more earlier in the year, but this was even more exciting and unique because Arla Williams had decided she was coming to Georgia to spend some time here and do a camp out with us.

There were a couple of areas very near our hunting property that I knew could be great if the forest friends were there, so one weekend Cathy and I drove out to some park areas located on a major river. We had just pulled into the

gates of one of those areas when immediately I knew this would be a great location for us. There were tree bows in sight with one pine pinned to the ground similar to one on our property and other "signs" that told me they were here. As we drove in, it was already in the late afternoon, so we wouldn't have but a very few hours to look around. That was all we needed as it turned out, we both found out they were indeed here.

We pulled into an area near a campground to which I was immediately drawn. I felt like they TOLD me "Stop your car here!" As we got out, I felt a sense of being in an area I had always known. It was somewhere that felt good and inviting. I felt like I just pulled into my grandparents' yard... just a very familiar and comfortable feeling. Cathy and I got out of the car and we were both overcome with a very strong odor that I immediately attributed to the trash cans located nearby.

I walked over to inspect the cans, expecting to see dead fish or something of the sort, but there was nothing and the smell had diminished. In just a few minutes, we

could not even smell it... which we thought odd.

Cathy and I began our walk down a horse trail that wound its way along a ridge. The trail was wide and well-traveled with horse traffic. As we walked on the trail, I heard sticks breaking under the weight of something and I immediately stopped. The sound was coming from a denser area down the ridge along a creek. I then caught a flash of brown and white moving fast headed towards us. As the sounds of a running animal grew closer, a whitetail doe burst out of the woods across the trail just a few feet from us. That startled us but was fun to watch.

We were laughing at being startled when we began to catch the same smell coming from the creek area the deer had just evacuated. Being a hunter, there were a few things that didn't make sense to me. The deer was running as if spooked, but was heading with the air current instead of against it. Normally a deer would flee and get the air current or breeze in its favor so they can smell what is ahead of them.

The other odd thing was that it ran straight up the hill, not along the ridge as I would have expected. I immediately knew that whatever spooked the deer was very close and most likely on the creek that was only fifty yards away and just at the bottom of the hill. The smell we had captured earlier was very strong there as well and the breeze was coming from the creek towards us. I told Cathy we should head back down the trail we came from as I knew there was another trail along the creek lower, I wanted to walk down it a ways to see if there was anything out of place or if, maybe, a track might be in the sandy areas on the trail.

Forest Friends of the Night

We returned to the car, got a drink and walked back towards the lower trail. This trail began just off the road and after a few steps, we came to a bridge that was built over the creek that crossed the trail. As we started over the bridge there were very distinct sounds in the leaves on the hill immediately to our right and along the side of the ridge to our left. There was just enough foliage to prevent us from seeing far either way. It was also getting close to dusk and the sun had already settled behind the hill. The woods had become very still and as we walked we could hear our footfalls very easily. Because it was a horse trail, there were not as many leaves as there were off the trail. We walked about fifty yards and we could both hear leaves rustling. We would stop and they would stop. This went on the entire time we were there. It was very obvious there was something there.

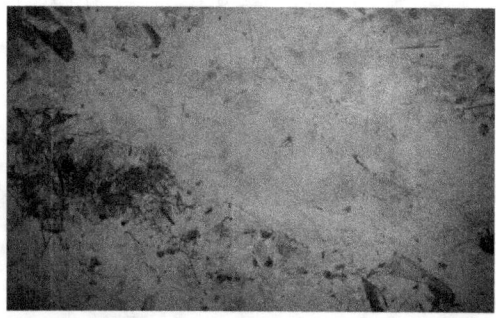

Both of us were wondering what we were going to see. As I was looking for movement on either side of me, Cathy exclaimed, "HEY! Look over here!"

I walked over and there was a very clear and obvious bare foot print in the sand. It was not extremely big and then we saw another ahead. The step was approximately five feet and the tracks around eleven inches long. Each print was aligned directly in front of the other, in a straight line. I tried to match the step and could not without jumping. Even when I jumped I still came up short. As we were looking Cathy also found very small tracks about four inches long. She then located a track about thirteen inches in length. It was just a single track this time.

We took photographs as the light was beginning to fade. We walked a bit further then decided we needed to head back because we didn't have a light and snakes were out that time of year. We turned and headed back and our "escort" walked with us. We talked to him like we knew who he was. "Hi there… We hear you. WE know you are walking with us."

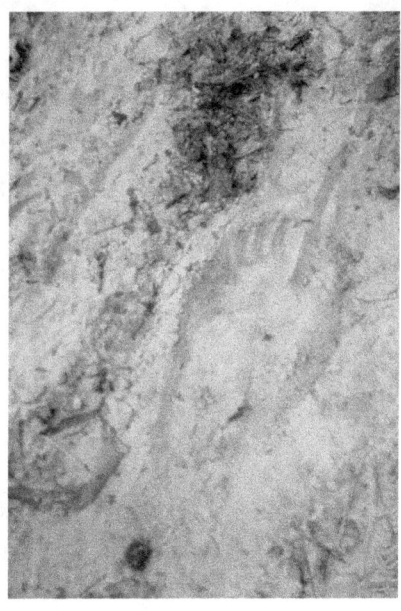

Forest Friends of the Night

At one point, I heard a grunt or something sounding like it. It was more than obvious they were there and both of us had the hair standing up on our necks. They walked with us all the way to the bridge and stopped as soon as we got there. As we turned, we both said, "goodbye friends," as the footsteps walked away this time, until they were gone from hearing.

We returned to the car too excited to leave, so we took a pair of chairs, and sat talking until the darkness of the night fully engulfed us. We sat a few feet away talking about what we had seen and heard for a very long time. After approximately thirty minutes, we were about to leave when we heard rustling in the leaves in front of where we were sitting. We spread out a few feet away and sat there, talking to each other and to whatever we heard. This time though, the sounds were ever so slight and my mind's eye told me it was an opossum or a raccoon.

I told Cathy we should probably go, when, all of a sudden, I heard what sounded like a rock being tossed between us. I laughing and said, "You missed me!"

A stick then came flying out of the trees and landed about a foot from me! I looked at Cathy and we laughed. After the last time, we waited a while and heard the footsteps walking away, so we decided to leave. We both told them, "goodbye and thank you!" WOW, I guess we found a GREAT place for Arla's gathering when she came to Georgia.

When we got home, I was thinking about what had happened... Again it was all so surreal! I called Arla and talked to her about all of this. We came to the conclusion there were obviously more than one of our visitors and, based on the tracks, a baby and at least one female and maybe a young male as well. There was a feeling with them as well... It was like they were very familiar.

I had many questions for Arla and Thom. Could they be the same from our hunting camp? It is less than ten miles away by the map. I had also heard they use travel routes and other ways of travel. The river and many power lines ran between our camp and this area as well. The answer was "absolutely, they could be the same ones."

That, to me was fascinating and one more great thing to know. As I found out later, this was a very special group of bigfoot people and I was to know them and others much better in the coming year and a half.

16. Back Home Again

After a couple of years in the new hunting area, we found out that our old property was available for lease again. We had been there since my high school days and had spent more than thirty years on that property camping and hunting. I spent some wonderful days with Dad and my family. To get the chance to return there was exciting!

After a couple of trips there, we saw there had been some major changes as the timber company had sold the hardwoods off it. With the exception of a fifty foot buffer strip along the creeks, the hardwoods that covered a third of the property were gone. The buffer rule was made to prevent trees around creeks and waterways from being cut to eliminate some of the issues which lead to erosion and dangerous waste water run off polluting creeks. That did help provide some food for the deer and other wildlife in the form of mast crops... acorns, a few walnut trees and hickory trees.

Forest Friends of the Night

The landscape had changed with the cutting of the hardwoods. That meant it could cause some differences in game movement as well as the amount of deer and other animals on the property. How would that affect the bigfoot? I was wondering about this and would soon find out.

We relocated our camp back to the old "home" site. It felt good to be back here. I was sad but a bit relieved when we left this site before because I had some fear of what was on the property. Now, I had a totally new perspective on the bigfoot people following our experiences during the last years.

As I drove across the property, it felt so different. I felt the bigfoot people would have had to change their hunting areas because we were going to have to do the same. I was also very concerned about the health of the deer herd there and wondered if the lack of acorns would play into the carrying capacity. Many times when populations of deer in areas get too high, nature has a way of bringing the population back under control. The dreaded Ephizootic Hemorrhagic Disease (EHD) also known as blue tongue has ravaged deer herds across the country when the population exceeds the carrying capacity... is too large for the available food sources.

Forest Friends of the Night

The cutting of hardwoods has also been very common for timber companies over the last few years due to the economic downturn. Paper sales and construction grade lumber sales have been reduced considerably. To help prevent that we began supplementing food as much as possible by creating as many food plots as we could. Also, we placed nutrient blocks and corn. We were doing what we could to increase the available food sources. We also placed game cameras on many of these areas to try to get an idea of how many deer were here.

The first night Cathy and I returned to that ground, I wondered how active the night would be. Prior to leaving, the nights here would come to life with sounds and activity. Standing outside on this warm night we had no need for a fire and we decided to sit a while and listen. For a while, we heard nothing but an occasional owl. Then, as we were thinking we wouldn't hear or experience anything, a low, deep howl emanated from along a hill across from camp and rose to a higher pitch. It lasted for only four or five seconds but it was definitely a sound I had heard before. I smiled and knew they were still here. We listened for a return and got it from a very long distance away, on the opposite side of the property. With that, we retired for the night and went inside, NOW it felt like home.

Forest Friends of the Night

As morning came so came the excitement of what the day would bring. The feeling of waking up to a beautiful sunrise and the forest coming to life never gets old. I headed out on my ATV to a familiar area with lots of memories. It was a place I had hunted many times and almost always saw many deer and was always alive with activity.

One morning, years prior, I watched a fascinating scene play out here. I was sitting along this same ridge looking down a draw and caught the movement of something black. As I looked I heard the familiar putt putt and purring of a hen turkey. I watched as a flock of turkeys were making their way across the ridge from me. All of a sudden, the lead hen started squawking out an alert call and the flock began running back and forth. I knew something scared them. As I was watched, I caught movement out of the corner of my eye as a coyote slipped underneath my stand heading very slowly down the hill. The turkeys were still cackling on the ridge and the coyote slowed as he got to within eighty yards where he then got on his belly and crawled across an opening to a fallen tree. He hid behind the tree peeking over it at the turkeys just up the hill. I then also saw another coyote on the hill moving slowly behind the turkeys. The turkeys began descending the hill in single file but walking fast toward the bottom where the other coyote lie in wait.

As soon as the turkey rounded the log, the coyote lunged and grabbed it by the neck. As it flapped its wings, the other turkeys went in all directions, some running some flying. As all of this was going on, the coyote on the hill along with another came trotting down the hill. They all began growling and pulling at the still flapping turkey. They then turned and trotted over the hill and all became quiet. Wow! What a moment to witness! I was thinking about how this scene has unfolded for hundreds of thousands of years.

After a few minutes the woods had settled down and I was about to leave my area and return to camp when I heard three distinct knocks....... whack, whack and whack... It was loud and close. It was within a hundred yards and was in the direction the coyotes had just gone. It was most definitely wood striking a tree. I knew the bigfoot People were close. Then I wondered, did they witness this too?

17. Arla and Friends Campout!

I proceeded back to the park that Cathy and I had visited for the planned campout that we had been planning. It was the weekend before the scheduled date and I wanted to make sure everything was in good order. I hoped to talk to the park attendants to make sure they knew we were coming. I also wanted to try to "connect" again with the bigfoot people there.

All that I have learned over the last years has taught me the one word that is the key to everything is "respect." I thought that I would go to the park and make sure they knew we were coming by doing what I felt would be respectful. I felt that if I let them know we were coming the next weekend it would be helpful.

Cathy and I walked back to the area we had found the tracks on our prior visit When I reached the little bridge we could hear the leaves on both sides rustling and obvious bipedal steps walking with us. We walked... they walked. We stopped... they stopped. It became readily apparent that this was a special area and it felt as if we had a private escort. We very simply walked in and stopped in the area I felt was where I needed to be and told them, "Hi Guys! We are back and I wanted to make sure all knew we were returning next weekend with new people. People are coming to camp to learn more about who you are." We heard no response, but assumed they heard us as I was sure the ones walking in with us were there for that purpose... then we left.

The next week began with lots of anticipation for the week. Arla and a few others were to arrive in the middle of the week and get everything set up. I had to fly out of town, but was trying to time my arrival back with Thom Cantrall who was flying into Atlanta on Wednesday night. As it turned out I had meetings that lasted longer than I wanted but I found him a ride from the airport to the Park via Cathy's sister. So, I arrived too late to meet him, but I was off the next two days from work and I was anxious to get there on the day following... on Thursday.

Since Cathy had to work and it was near the area we were camping, we opted to get a hotel room between the park and her office. I got to the hotel, checked in and went out to greet my friends. I pulled in to see Arla and Thom and a few others gathered around. The weather was gorgeous with highs in the seventies and lows in the upper fifties at night. By ones and twos throughout the day people arrived. We had approximately ten on Thursday with more scheduled to arrive on Friday and Saturday.

Already Arla, Gail and our Friend Jonathan had found some structures and glyphs in the area. Thom and Arla are both experienced with glyphs and I longed to learn more about them. The ones found were obviously manipulated and, because of the nature of that, it was easy to tell they were not  naturally occurring... yet another wonderful mystery of the bigfoot people. What are they and what do they mean? That is something I yield to other, more studied experience and not my own, but I am astounded by them.

Thursday evening grew near and the air was cooling to usher in a magnificent night. As it was getting near dark,

Forest Friends of the Night

my wife Cathy arrived and many of us were making little mini excursions into the woods that surrounded our area. Again, anticipation was running high for what might happen. Most were sitting around the fire and we were having a grand time talking. There were many personal experiences that were too numerous for me to mention here, but suffice it to say the night was interesting. Cathy and I had to leave as she was working earlier but I was anxious to hear the stories from the night before.

The next day Cathy readied herself for work and I got dressed and did a little work on my laptop before heading to the campout. When I arrived, I was shown tracks behind someone's truck where bigfoot walked into camp! Many heard them walking around the tents and one person had actually seen one looking into his tent window! This person said something to him and he moved away from the window to the front of the tent! There were some great stories and that was only the

first night. How much better was this going to get?

Many more people arrived in the next few hours leading into the late afternoon. Tents were being raised while the excitement level grew from the stories being shared by the ones that had experiences. As the group had grown substantially from the night before, so did the amount of people circling the fire. Good times, good food and good stories were being shared. Then again as the night approached, the excitement level was high! As dusk approached a few of us walked past our camp down a little path that started as the driveway in. The path was a horse trail that wound through the woods and there were so many bowed trees, as well as other tree structures that appeared not naturally made. In one instance, a large "X" was made with two very large pine trees. They were so large, in fact, that it would have taken considerable strength to bend them to their places. There were two stumps that matched the break line of the tree bases. One was located about ten feet away from the tree it matched while the other was about five feet. It was apparent they were dragged to their final location and assembled into the shape of the "X."

As I made my way back into camp with the others, Arla and Jonathan had been walking as well. They actually had a visual of one crossing the road in front of them! Jonathan took me to the spot and showed me... Things were definitely getting interesting!

It was totally dark by the time we arrived back in camp. I wanted to show Thom and a few more the area I like to walk where the two "escorts" follow me. We loaded into my truck and I first drove them to the river area of the park to show the lay of the property there. As we were driving by the river, there was another truck headed our way and we met on the little dirt road area. It was the Park Ranger that lived there and he was making sure we were okay and all was fine as there were not too many people camping that were still up and about. We assured him we were and I told him we were simply taking in the night sounds. He then told me, "Well, you may hear some sounds here you have never heard before."

I laughed and began to drive off, then I thought about the fact I never told them why we were actually there. I stopped, opened the window and asked him, "Exactly what kind of sounds?"

"Well," he said, "there are things here that make some different sounds." That is when I told him who we were and why we were there. He chuckled and said, "Well, there very well could be some bigfoot around!"

Forest Friends of the Night

I pulled the truck into the same little area Cathy and I parked the week before and we headed into the area where we normally get escorted. We got to the bridge and I had brought a parabolic microphone with me this time. We crossed the bridge and again, we heard them walking us in just like every time we have been here. This time it was easier to hear them. I let a couple of the others hear as well. We walked down the trail and once we got to the area where I normally stop, we could hear footfalls around us.

One of my friends had a digital recorder and we placed it in a good location next to the trail. Many of the researchers that I know believe that recorders are not something the bigfoot mind being used in their area. We were not going to take photos if we got a visual. I firmly believe they don't like it. I certainly don't want to disrespect them in any way. We left and headed back to camp.

Upon returning, we sat and talked for a while. A few of our number had gone out hiking so I was anxious to hear what they experienced. In a bit they returned and, although they hadn't seen anything, there were lots of noises around and as they were sitting in the woods, a tree fell very close to them. This is another part of the bigfoot repertoire, either for communication to others or something else, this is a common occurrence when around them.

Cathy was tired from work, so we headed back to the hotel for some rest, but the next morning we returned early to prepare for speakers we had planned for the many people that drove in for the one day speaker and dinner event. Many more people were there and they too were entertained but the new stories from the night time visitors. Again, they were around the tents and even around the food tent making noise. There was lots of excitement just before the speakers began and the excitement would definitely continue throughout the day.

Arla led off with a prayer song and then a great presentation. Thom then followed and another great presentation. We then broke for lunch. As we were taking our break, Arla and some of the others were helping get food set up and called a few of us over. They had left a frying pan that was washed from the earlier breakfast sitting on the propane stove. In the pan was a leaf with a crystal rock placed on top of it! That had been placed there while we were just across the dirt road in the speaker's area!

Again, I got to see something astounding! I was thinking about that as we returned to finish our speaker's part of the campout. After the speakers, we had a nice Barbecue dinner. We then gathered around the fire, readying ourselves for the stories and another night of fun!

As evening fell and the dusk fast approached, we were sharing stories from the many great people and researchers gathered. It was then that two of the ladies got very excited! One was pointing behind where we were sitting and was said with a quivering lip, "We're not alone... LOOK! There is one right there!"

I quickly turned to look, as did a couple of others and saw the branches of a tree move as something rapidly moved past it. Jennifer and Annette were still there as Annette yelled, "He was standing right there! Neither of them had ever had a visual sighting so excitement was an understatement!

Arla then stood up and very slowly began walking towards them. I could hear her soft voice saying: "Hi Guys how are you?" It was like a Mom would have talked to one of her kids that had just walked in the front door. She was kind and reassuring as she continued walking towards where the branch had moved.

I got up as well and went with her as I wanted to get a better look. I still had not had a good visual, just glimpses. We were joined by Jonathan and Gail. I was beside Arla and she told me, "Keith, there is one just in front of me, look towards your left, he is a small guy."

I looked in the direction and I could see a dark patch, but it was hidden in the trees about ten feet way. Then I heard Arla say: "Oh, there is a big guy there too... he is huge!"

I then saw a larger black mass in the shadows and I could see an arm move then a leg and it seemed to vanish into the shadows… Oh My. I couldn't believe what I had just seen.

In all of the excitement I noticed one of the boys that had come with his dad was there too. I turned to ask if he saw them.

He said, "I saw something big!"

We continued trying to see. Arla and Jonathan had moved to my left and ahead of us. It was clear that Arla was still seeing them and Jonathan then said, "I see him!" I walked towards Jonathan and he said, "Look between those two trees!"

I could see a dark figure that appeared to be swaying, ever so slightly back and forth. This continued as the last remaining minutes of daylight disappeared, carrying with it the last images of them moving around. We then turned and I walked back to the fire in a complete daze. I was shaking with excitement. Jonathan and eleven year old Zach were excited too. Zach went to tell his Dad and we all simply sat there amazed at what had just happened. After a bit, I was so in awe of my experience I was drained. My life if not changed totally before, was now changed.

As hours had passed, many other exciting things had happened. One of the other guys had removed the digital recorder he brought and would review it later when he was back at home. From all the activity, I felt sure something was there. The night grew late and I felt drained from all of the excitement.

We were about to head home and we were saying goodbye to some that would leave early when I heard Zach tell his dad, "Dad, we have seen more bigfoot in two days than Bobo on Finding Bigfoot has in two seasons!"

18. They are a People

The weekend Cathy and I shared in Georgia was simply amazing. The activity and visuals that we had were something that I had never expected. I knew they were in the area and I knew they were active there so my hope was for some night time vocals or maybe find tracks or other "sign" of them to share with the ones coming to learn more. I also knew many of the people who would be attending had a long history of experience. They had heard the stories, shared pictures, and fellowship. The experience would be great. As it turned out, everyone that attended had experiences that were either life changing or, at the least, would be lifelong memories.

The next few weeks for me were a time for reflection... deep thought and trying to put it all together. Why was this such a powerful experience? Was there more to the learning aspect of this from the bigfoot people to us? That would be my focus over the next year as it seems there was a lesson in this to me and I am sure to others that were there.

In the short period of a couple of years, I had gone from being a somewhat skeptical believer to a "knower". I had not only had confirmed visuals, but so had my wife and many of the people that came to the gathering. Trying to find answers to the questions I had poised in my mind, I became much more active on the internet and on social group pages in groups that my other friends were in. We shared things that happened. I asked questions and there was never a shortage of feedback.

Many of the larger groups had so many skeptics and people making fun of others, us and me that it was impossible to enjoy them. Why is this so very emotional? I wanted to share with friends and family and began to get very frustrated with people making fun of it and rolling eyes. I am the type of person that has never been prone to just make up stories or lies and still this happened time and time again. There were times I was simply depressed at the fact my very own blood kin made light of the whole thing, poking fun at my expense. Then, after much talking to Arla and others that went through this, I got to the point that I was not going to let them get to me. What happened was real... it was also shared with many others. My resolve and determination began to grow. I decided I was going to be myself, share with others that want to hear and try to not let it bother me. Surrounding me with others that wanted to share was like a prescribed medicine. I got stronger and more determined, other friendships grew from this.

Some that I met over the next few months were like me... eager to learn and hear more so I began sharing. Since I had become friends with so many in the community, it helped me as I began to share through interviews. I began to put these together through the blog site I helped operate.

All of the information shared from the great people I had come to know was making me understand that I was not in this by myself. I wanted to help the bigfoot people by trying to make others see that they are not "monsters", they are a people. Thus my "mission" to them began in earnest. I would also point out to others the data that was coming to light almost daily. The results of a five year DNA study was but one example of that fact.

The Sasquatch Genome Project was well underway when I began my investigations. It was a five year study that concluded with some mixed reviews. I had become part of a social group that at one time would try and help prove the sasquatch or bigfoot people, as they are variously called, to science. Our goal was to raise awareness of them and maybe help protect them. This I would later change my opinion entirely. In short, the DNA investigation group that was headed by Dr. Melba Ketchum was to submit to a major science journal to get them listed as a real species. This faltered at the end of the study during the peer review process mostly due to the fact that established science would not accept something that so radically opposed their own preconceived notions of what was. Even though there were well over a hundred samples including hair, saliva, blood, tissue and even a toenail that had been obtained my many researchers and submitted from all over North America, it was not sufficient for the reviewers.

Laboratories utilized in this study included three major universities, University of Southern California, University of Texas and Texas A&M University, Dr. Ketchum's

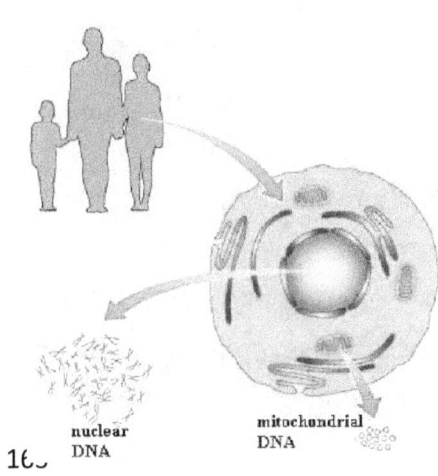

nuclear DNA

mitochondrial DNA

163

Forest Friends of the Night

Alma Mater. The results were then forwarded on to Dr Ketchum to collate the results and make final conclusions on the project. She also wrote the report for the journal along with all photos, videos and other pertinent evidence. The conclusions were amazingly similar and resulted in a "unknown" in the Nuclear DNA (nuDNA). The nuDNA is a combination of DNA from the two parents. In each chromosome pair, one half comes from the father and one half from the mother. This nuDNA, as the name implies, is found in the nucleus of the atom.

The Mitochondrial DNA (mtDNA) from all humans is contained within the mitochondria of the cell and comes to us from our matrilineal line... from our mothers, grandmothers, great grandmothers and so on back to the beginning. This mtDNA was found to be one hundred percent human. It is only one quarter of one percent of the total DNA found in the cell and the coding is for thirty seven genes and contains sixteen thousand six hundred base pairs inherited solely from the mother.

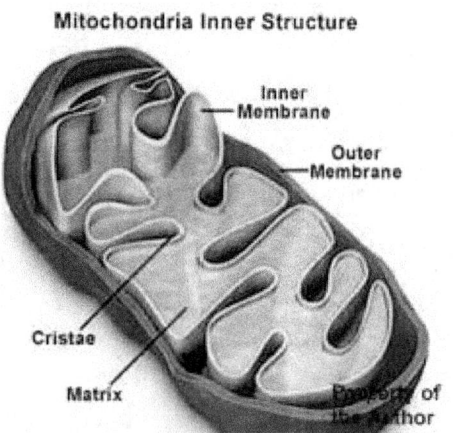

Mitochondria Inner Structure

Inner Membrane

Outer Membrane

Cristae

Matrix

The nuDNA encompasses ninety nine and three quarters percent of the cell DNA and contains information from one copy from each parent. This can be linked directly to a parent or lineage whereas the mtDNA can only be linked to the mother's lineage.

All DNA testing is contained in a database called Gen Bank. It is common practice to compare tested DNA to data contained in the Gen Bank files and from this, the source of the tested DNA can be determined. The five markers the Genome Project identified in the nuDNA that are different from our own were also unknown in Gen Bank and cannot be linked to anything there. This in itself is a very interesting result, but even this was scoffed at because the peer review panel simply could not understand this anomaly. Why would they do this?

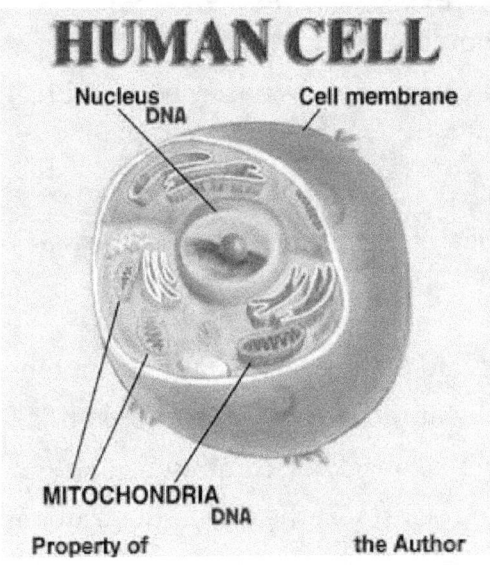

HUMAN CELL

Nucleus
DNA

Cell membrane

MITOCHONDRIA
DNA

Property of   the Author

Forest Friends of the Night

After the journal did not publish the findings, I soon changed my entire thinking to I NEVER want them discovered by science. The reason became clear once I thought about what would happen. They would not be accepted as people right away. Too many years of being stereotyped as monsters, wild animals and evil beings would prevent that. The thoughts of people fearing them and possibly going out looking for them armed is made worse by knowing lots of people would now be endangered by some scared and crazed person wanting to kill one. Even worse, the Government would get involved. That would make things totally worse for everyone concerned! So, I feel as though by the study not being accepted by a major journal was actually a very good thing. The results can be found online at; http://sasquatchgenomeproject.org/view-dna-study/.

Many other factors had testified to me as far as them being a type of person. The apple story from earlier in this book showed me they can reason. They communicated to me by helping me find the rock stack, the tree in the trail and feathers left with rocks on them. I think they communicate to themselves by the many tree structures that we find. The tree knocks, howls and other verbal utterances such as what Ron Morehead and Scott Nelson has been working on are further illustrations of intelligent communication. The glyphs that Thom, Arla and Brian Bland are all working on indicate there is language present. There is also much more I have learned from others through interactions I have heard and now experienced that there is no doubt we are dealing with a very intelligent being.

19

-- Glyphs –

The Written Language of Sasquatch
Chronicles of the Alpha Project

By

Thom Cantrall

With Brian Bland and Sue Funkhouser

The rain had eased off to a mere mist as the two men carefully moved around the large structure they had been

directed to in a remote corner of British Columbia, Canada. Rain was a common feature here and was certainly no stranger to these two. The wooden structure they had just located was unique, however, and, while they were in an area that other people could certainly have reached, the probability of that was low, so, what had made this device they now marveled over?

As we looked this asterisk shaped structure over carefully, we found that the logs used in its construction had not grown there. They had been moved there and placed in the orientation seen in the photograph. No signs of human presence were found. We photographed the area extensively, made such notes as we felt appropriate and retreated from this area. We could return to this at any time we so felt it necessary. In fact, we do return often because of its special beauty and significance.

We investigated the area thoroughly and feel with a high degree of confidence in our decision to attribute this to the native population of this area. Can we say with one hundred percent certainty that this is the work of the sasquatch people that reside here? No, we cannot, but with our investigations of the circumstances and the area, I am more than ninety nine percent

"H" Glyph

certain that this is the case.

With this experience we formed a loose coalition to investigate and study these structures. We would later find a name for this group, but at the time of this discovery in

2012, "Project Alpha" had not yet been heard of officially. We were just Thom 'n Tot, the two guys doing that study project on sasquatch writing.

Today, going into the fourth year of this study, we can look back with a degree of detachment on the journey we have been taking. At this time of our inception, we knew of no others who were doing this same work anywhere in the world. I would assume there had to be some who were interested enough to be doing this, but I'm certainly not sure of that.

While we were fascinated by the structures and glyphs we were finding, today, we understand how elementary they actually were. It was like they

started us off with printing such as we'd learn in our primary grades in school... most glyphs were strictly two dimensional... there was no Z axis to them.

During this time of learning, we came to understand that there were classes of glyphs we were finding. Most commonly we found that the great majority of these were not for our use, purpose or understanding. They were a communications form they used among themselves. We have estimated that nearly eighty five percent of all that we find falls into this category. Of the remaining fifteen percent, there are distinct categories with "Signature" glyphs being the most common.

Two of the most commonly found glyphs that fall into this category were the "H" glyph and the "4" glyph. The H, we discovered, was the signature of the daughter of the clan leader. Rahjahsay was a young woman at this time and very shortly thereafter took a mate, Forshnah. The 4 is his signature. Please understand this did not leap out at us... we did not know it intuitively. It was the result of much study and contemplation of thousands of photographs of their glyphs.

Forest Friends of the Night

Authentication became a very big deal for us in our work. It seemed that almost immediately upon sharing our work with others, the haters came out of the woodwork. People who lack the imagination to see what we see or lack the initiative to even look for this began attacking us personally and our work in general. We were "reading tea leaves..." We were making them ourselves... they were simply the work of natural wind and weather... all of these charges were leveled at us with some vehemence in many cases. I wondered if they actually believed that we might not suspect that there are other forces that could be at work here. Could we actually be ignoring the fact that it's possible for humans to make these glyphs? Were we so ignorant that we would not assess the possibility of other aspects of the possibilities here?

The FIRST thing we do is assume it could be one of these factors that created these works... then we went to work to find clues to authenticate them. We searched for clues diligently... While not always easily found, clues do exist... some are evident and others less so. Some are more compelling than others, but the fact is, they are evidence.

On occasion, we have even been fortunate enough to find a glyph made directly adjacent to a footprint, or, more rarely, a larger glyph with a trackway directly through the glyph. Occasionally, we are blessed with a glyph made in a track... when we find these, it is generally a very significant

16" track adjacent to simple direction glyph

type of glyph. Most often it is some form of direction glyph, another category of glyph we find often enough to designate it with its own classification.

Although direction glyphs take many forms, they are seldom meant for us, but are part of that eighty five percent that are for their use and understanding. Sometimes they are simply arrows and at others, they are like a T with, I believe, the direction of travel indicated by the blunt or cross part of the T.

The "naturally occurring" people turn up often... "Oh, this is just the result of winds blowing them this way..." If that were so, what would be the odds of finding this?

Forest Friends of the Night

These three triangle glyphs were found over two years and were many miles apart. British Columbia certainly must have consistent winds, huh? Anyone who can argue that these are random and a work of the wind... well, I have a bridge for sale he might be interested in. I must point out that this is only a FEW of this glyph... we must have fifteen or so pictures of this structure taken across many miles of B.C. and Washington.

The year 2013 held some new surprises for us. First, they raised the ante to play the game. Early in the year, we started finding some new wrinkles in our glyph deciphering hat. A Z-Axis was introduced... now, suddenly, we were finding glyphs

constructed in three dimensions... not only were they left and right, up and down, but now they came off the page at us! It was as if we had just graduated from kindergarten printing to third grade cursive writing! We had arrived! Of course, we now understood even less of what we were seeing, but it did open a whole new world to us!

The glyph displayed here has some further significance to it as well as being the first really Three-D glyph found. It is made of branches from a birch tree. In this area of British Columbia, birch trees grow only in the river and creek bottoms... not three miles up a side hill above

Glyph found under our tent guy

the river where this as found in the snow. Also, there are no tracks around it even though it was obviously made after the last snowfall or there would be snow ON the branches as well. There is not. Further, this was not in an area where humans would attend at this time of year or could not without leaving a trackway of their own. No such trackway was encountered.

In this structure, the branch that is running from the right and up at forty five degrees toward the left is buried deeply in the snow. The other two are merely placed on top of that cross member to give the lift that keeps it off the snow. These last two pieces are stuck into the snow only far enough to keep them in place on the structure.

In July of this year, we, as a team, attended Todd Neiss's "Beachfoot" gathering in Waldport, Oregon. We were asked to give a presentation on this subject which we willingly did... even though it met with skepticism from some quarters and total rudeness and disdain from a couple of people. It mattered not to us as we are quite used to people with little to no experience in the sasquatch phenomenon being the most difficult to show simple respect for another's effort.

While a couple of people were disdainful, most of those attending found it interesting at least and compelling at times. Several people came to us to tell of finding similar structures... even while here at the gathering. Some took us to places they had encountered exactly what we were speaking of at our presentation. The ultimate waited until our last morning there. It was after our presentation...

Upon arising that last morning, one of my tent mates decided it was time to start breaking camp... at least somewhat... to that end, she decided to remove the rain fly from over our tent. When she went to the end to remove the stake and line that held it in place, a new glyph was there... it had NOT been there the night before... this stake was just outside the door of one of our colleague's tent and she would have noticed any such thing. Notice that the large stick is distending the tie down cord for the rain fly... and it is over the sticks that make up part of the glyph... none of us have any idea what the meaning of this is other than to just let us

"Thom" glyph from BC, Canada

know they were there. The timing would so indicate.

There were, of course naysayers and detractors concerning this, but I have learned to ignore the fools and just go ahead. No one ever created anything worthwhile by listening to detractors.

A month later, I was in camp with a crew of people, including our Project Team Member, Sue, at a place in Oregon we had dubbed Camp Broken Arrow. CBA is in the Cascade Mountains of Oregon, southwest of Mt. Hood. The spot was beautiful and activity was rampant. We had nightly visitations from the big people... even had them walking through camp and talking. One of the stranger manifestations occurred while we were not in camp.

Forest Friends of the Night

One facet of the signature glyphs that became quite personal was when we discovered they had a glyph used to signify us. Above is my personal identity glyph which was found in B.C., Canada.

One afternoon in Oregon, we decided as a group to drive around the area and see what we could discover. The

"Thom" glyph from CBA, Oregon

drive took much of our day as there was much to see and do in this beautiful area of Oregon and no one was very anxious to miss it. All ten people in camp were with us on this outing, no one was left behind. The camp was empty when we left and when we returned, the tracks in the road leading in to our spot told us no other vehicle nor individual had entered the area in our absence.

Forest Friends of the Night

On returning to camp, I was quite tired. I had been undergoing some rigorous health adjustments and this trip started out very difficult for me. When I landed out of Jim's little truck, I immediately started for my chair that was under the sun fly near our fire pit. I sat down and relaxed while I waited  for the others to join me for conversation, likely about what we had seen on our outing. As I relaxed there, I allowed my eyes to drift downward and there, on the ground near my feet was a glyph... MY glyph...

I was totally astounded by this event. I sat in awe of what I was seeing. Here... over three hundred miles from where we found the original, I was looking at its virtual twin!

 The quality and complexity of their glyphs continues to increase. Every time out we find more intricate and

179

interesting designs. They seem to know no bounds to the art they perform as they continue to amaze those of us on this Alpha Project.

When we started, no one was talking about or, really, looking for glyphs... there were a few who knew what they were, but only THE few... this has changed now. Today there are people in many states across the land who are recording and chronicling the appearance of these enigmatic forms. We have watchers from Florida, Georgia, and all parts of the Southeastern area of the country through the Midwest... the mountain west as well as California, north to Canada.

Our research goes on... we continue to find more and learn more. We hope to be able to decipher the meanings of more and more of these beautiful structures as time goes along. Today, we have over fifteen thousand photographs of glyphs and add to it regularly. What is coming? We have no idea, but it's going to be a fun trip in finding out!

20. The Night the Lights Went On in GA

The spring following our Georgia campout we began to discuss trying to have another, but it was not going to be possible to get everyone back here. There was a group of people that was not able to attend the fall campout so wanted to camp anyway. To accommodate them, I scheduled a few days at the end of a week in May with the park that had helped us with a very successful gathering last year. We would have four men and some children camping for two nights. Cathy and I would come in on Saturday and stay from early in the day through the night. I would take them to the same location as I took the other group.

The weekend came and the group of guys showed up and camped Thursday and Friday nights. The same type of experiences with some howls, lots of movement in and around camp and other events occurred. My wife and I arrived there on Saturday evening. After introductions to those I had not met, we sat around the fire, shared some stories and grilled some steaks for dinner. The night was great and so was the company. All was completely relaxing and normal... Until later when we would then witness something that I cannot explain. It was a completely extraordinary event that I will never forget.

In this journey of the last few years, I have learned to expect the unexpected and keep an open mind. I will admit though, there have been a few times I would hear of something the bigfoot people do such as cloaking, or having eye shine at night with no light source that I have had a very hard time accepting. This night I would become a total believer that there are things they can do that simply defy logic as I know it. When I was at the Southeastern conference that Alex Munoz hosted in January of 2013, I witnessed eye shine on the hill behind the conference center. I could see "eyes" doing something similar to what you would see deer eyes do when a light reflected off them. These were moving and some were too high to be deer. We could hear bipedal foot falls for a very long time. This was fascinating but I could not one hundred percent verify this was not something else. So here is the story of what happened and witnessed by all five of us:

Forest Friends of the Night

It was Saturday evening May sixteenth, 2014... a very nice, warm night in Georgia. Five of us took a short drive in my truck down to the area where I have had my encounters. My wife stayed at camp with the kids as they were afraid to go into the woods at night. We parked next to a family at a camp ground and were enjoying the night out by the fire. I walked over to let them know we were going to have a little night walk in the woods just so they were not spooked by five men walking around in the dark.

We introduced ourselves and one lady told us, "We have been hearing weird noises in those woods. It sounds like a crying baby in there and we were worried someone might be in there lost. We were about to call the Ranger."

I told her we would have a look to make sure all was okay. At nine thirty pm, we entered the trail the same as I have many times before. The moon had not risen yet and there were a few high, thin clouds causing it to be much darker than usual. I kept the flashlight pointed down, so as to only help find rocks sticking up in the trail. We turned the light out as much as possible because all I had heard about the bigfoot people told me they don't like flashlights. I wanted to respect that.

We were met at the bridge and we could very clearly hear them walking on both sides of us. I let my companions use the parabolic to hear them very clearly. We walked in very slowly and stopped every fifty feet or so. There began to be sounds like talking but very low and barely audible. We could hear them better with the parabolic but couldn't make out words. It was on both sides and ahead of us, moving back and forth. Once we got to the area I normally go to and stopped, we heard a very loud and distinct whistle behind us. We turned and retreated a few feet in the direction of the whistle. There was a shuffling of leaves all around, when we noticed a light on the hill across from where we stood. At first, we thought the light was a flashlight or maybe two of them on the hill. The lights began to move down the hill towards us... Was it someone coming down the hill with lights?

We waited and watched, and the lights began to dim little by little as they got closer. Now there were two lights six to eight inches apart. Again the lights were moving down the hill. We could hear the footfalls getting closer and then I realized that walk down the hill is super treacherous and very thick to maneuver. That is NOT a person!

Whatever it was was now standing thirty feet away from us and the lights were not lights but eyes! We could very clearly see it blinking and he was very tall! He was swaying back and forth while looking over a branch that we later measured at nine feet high. We were looking at him as he was looking back and still moving back and forth.

All of a sudden Jason, one of my friends, let out a grunting sound. The eyes turned from a yellowish white to bright red-orange color! "WOW," I exclaimed, "JASON, DON'T DO THAT AGAIN HE IS UPSET!!"

As he stood there the feeling of calm changed to fright and we all were a little nervous. I told the bigfoot very quickly, "I am very sorry, we won't do that again!"

We stood a few more minutes and his eyes slowly changed back to a white color. He then turned and walked back up the hill and towards the end of the draw along the creek. We stood there shaking with excitement and completely shocked by what had just happened.

Forest Friends of the Night

We all saw it too for several minutes. After we calmed down, we decided it was time to return to the truck so we turned and began walking out again, very slowly. After a few feet I saw something move off the side of the trail... AGAIN EYES! They were right off the trail, not more than twenty feet. Another set of eyes appeared even closer. They were not more than ten feet away and very low to the ground. The closer one jumped up and ran through the woods extremely fast while jumping over the creek with a thud. We kept walking and were escorted all the way back out to the bridge. We could hear then walk away as we stood there trembling from excitement.

We rode back to camp and of course we were all very excited about what had happened. I have seen for myself and had verified by four others they do have a way to make their eyes shine without a light. I will admit that, for a few seconds, I was scared when we saw him react to the grunt that Jason made. Overall, however, we were not afraid but were simply excited. We told my wife the story and were exhausted by the events that were so incredible.

Later, as I lay in bed, I was totally shocked at this latest event. I am now totally open to what they can do. Seeing is believing and it was not just me but all five of us who saw. I have since read many more stories of this same phenomenon. I have also seen people get beat up by skeptics on the forums and other social media. This is one that I have not shared with others either until this book.

I researched animals that could do this and quickly learned there are species of fish that occupy the deepest reach of the oceans that can also do this. So, biologically, it happens and is possible. In order to learn, we have to be open to possibilities!

21. Fun and Games

The next year we were planning our second annual "Arla's Bigfoot Laidback Georgia Gathering" campout. Before October arrived, we spent time getting our hunting property ready and checking our deer cameras as well as laying out winter food plots. One of our hunters had put out nutrition blocks to help  give the deer extra minerals and vitamins to help them grow healthy during the summer. This allowed them to gain extra fat and nutrients to aide in antler growth as well as helping them get ready for the upcoming breeding season and winter.

One evening while standing around a late summer campfire, he brought up something very puzzling. The following is a paraphrase of what he told us regarding his observations on one of his game cameras. He had returned from the field and loaded the SD card into his laptop. He was scrolling through his pictures of the deer feeding on the nutrient block. There were many night photos of deer coming and going. As he was clicking through the pictures he noticed that, because the timer was set every minute or so and because of the solid positioning on the tree, playing them back made it look like a slow motion movie.

He was watching a buck eating around the block and all of a sudden, between one picture and the next, the deer had disappeared and so had the block. The block weighed between thirty and forty pounds and was located in a dense pine thicket. He was completely startled by what had happened.

He was new to our property and I had never told him anything about the bigfoot people being in the area because I didn't want it to cause any alarm. They had always been there and many never even knew they were around.

October was fast approaching and we had put together the same type of campout as the year before. Many that attended last year were coming back because of all of the excitement. I made sure the park and the park management knew about us. Again, Cathy with two of our grandsons, Hunter and Leithen drove out with me the weekend before to touch bases and make sure they knew we were going to be there.

As I drove up to the gate, I announced to the girl working the gate house, who I was. She exclaimed, "Oh your one of those bigfoot people!"

"They told me ya'll were coming again."

She walked out to the car and we engaged in a short conversation. She asked, "Are they real?"

I told her, "Of course they are!"

She simply laughed at me and said "Okay!"

Later, one of the older gentlemen that worked there last year saw me and drove over on his golf cart so we could talk. He told me of a story of bigfoot people they had seen around his house a few miles from there. He was a believer and knew they were around the park too. So, he told me, "They are still occasionally seen by people, but many don't say much because I think they are afraid people wouldn't believe them."

He said they always get reports of noises and sounds at night so I invited him to come down to our camp one night and he said he would.

Forest Friends of the Night

The park was hosting The Boy Scouts of America Camporee there that weekend and there was also a Native American Pow Wow under way. Needless to say, there were tents everywhere. I simply smiled knowing the bigfoot people love to people watch so they would be busy with the antics they would be seeing in the park. It seemed they rather enjoy it anyway and I think it is another reason they stay around the area. There were still hundreds of thousands of acres outside the boundaries of the four hundred acre park for them anyway.

We arrived at the area of the wooden bridge and we walked in with the boys. Hunter and Leithen were walking with me down the trail and were arguing the fact if the bigfoot people were real or not. As we walked down the trail I asked Leithen why he didn't believe.

He said; "they are pretend monsters"

I corrected him and told him, "No, they are a type of people that live in the woods."

He asked, "Can I talk to them then?"

I told him, "Sure you can. Just ask them if they are real, maybe they will respond."

Forest Friends of the Night

He asked them, "Are there any bigfoot out here?"

After a minute or two of silence, Leithen said, "See? I told you they are not real!"

I told him, "They may not be at home right now."

As soon as I said that, we heard a series of knocks on a tree... RAP, RAP, RAP.

Leithen looked at me and I told him, "See? They answered you!"

He shook his head no, and said, "That was a 'tapping bird.'"

I asked what a tapping bird was and he said, "The ones that make holes in trees!"

I laughed and then we heard a very loud RAP, RAP. I then asked, "Is that a tapping bird?"

He said, "I don't know... it'd have to be a big one!"

Forest Friends of the Night

We laughed and walked back out down the trail. We returned and built a little fire at the camp site and cooked hot dogs. All was quiet for the rest of the night and things seemed still except for kids we could hear playing in the distance. This was a quite weekend, but the next weekend was going to be different!

22. Seeing Is Believing

The weekend of our next gathering was fast approaching. Many that had attended the previous year were returning. The anticipation of the weekend was in motion from last year's occurrences as it had turned into a grand event and this one would, we were sure, be even better.

Gail arrived on site several days early as she was camping in our area. She began having activity from the first night.

Arla left Oklahoma on her drive with her dog Wado. Together they picked up Thom as he flew into Little Rock, Arkansas to meet them and to travel together.

We had people coming in from Colorado, California, Kentucky, Tennessee, Florida, Washington and many areas of Georgia. Cathy and I were on our way from a mini vacation in Florida and we would be staying at home this week instead of camping because of Cathy's work schedule. I drove to camp around noon on Thursday and stayed until later in the evening. I would then begin working on barbecue pork for Friday night's dinner.

Events were planned and hopefully our big friends would be around for the entertainment of watching the crazy people around the fire later.

Jonathan Gobles

Upon arriving, and I set up a tent for friends that would be coming in later. I found that a few were out on hikes. And, as I was standing in camp I looked across the field adjacent to us and a couple of the lady researchers were coming back to camp. As they got half way across the field, I noticed movement behind them towards the edge of the woods. I at first thought it was someone in all black with a hooded jacket, but I then saw the figure run up to a pine tree just in front of the wood line. I watched the tree closely until, about a minute later, it stepped out in the open, broad daylight and took a few steps and was gone back into the woods! It was not nearly as big as others I had seen, but was about six feet tall with long, slim arms. I got a great look as it was not more than one hundred yards off and was visible for several seconds.

I introduced myself to Robin and Brenda, the two who had just walked through the field. I asked if they had any experiences while on their hike.

Robin said, "Yes! I caught the glimpses of a black colored bigfoot walking behind us. He followed us for quite a distance."

I left a bit after this to go home and prepare the meat for the next day's barbecue.

I returned during afternoon with the barbecue I had cooked all morning. There had been some rather strong storms that had come through in the early morning, leaving slightly cooler weather.

We had also had our first injured member of any of our outings as Scott and his brother Farrell's tent's awning had received damage and he ended up with a cut finger trying to get it fixed. All others seemed fine and we ended up having a glorious meal. There were lots of good stories and Arla sang a prayer song as we sat around the fire. I left a little early as I had to get ready for our next day of fun and finish the presentation I was to do in the morning.

The day went by quite quickly and after the presentations were given by our speakers, we had a group of boy scouts show up. It turned out that the park staff had told them about us.

A member, Darrin, had brought Raven, his eight foot tall bigfoot mockup he had constructed. Many people loved getting photographs with him. That was enjoyable, but we would have even more fun later.

We had another guest join us from California. He is quite active in many projects in the outdoors. I can only use his initials here to protect his identity. DM had been to last year's event and had many experiences but did not have a visual sighting. This time, we were hoping that he would. We had a couple that lived locally and visited us during the day. They are friends and they have a very active area just down the road from our gathering. They had been having frequent visitors to their home almost nightly and because of who this group represented, they had extended an offer that anyone who wished to go out to their home would be welcome. DM and others decided to do just that and left for what would turn out to be a life changing moment for him.

After dark Arla, Cathy, Scott, Gail and I headed over to the area of the bridge to see if the BF People were there as they had almost always been. Since Scott was new, I explained to him what to expect as far as the escorts that would walk with us from the bridge into the area that I visit and communicate with them. The night was lighter than normal as he had a big, bright, nearly full moon shining down from above. We could catch glimpses of movement from time to time as shadows darted in and out of the trees. I gave Scott the parabolic microphone and he was in awe of them walking with us. He could also hear other sounds they make at a lower frequency range.

Like always, we were greeted with the bipedal footsteps in the leaves on both sides of us. We walked in

The Bridge

slowly with our flashlights pointed at the ground. When we

got to my normal area, we heard some sticks breaking and heavy foot falls coming from a big hill on our right side and in front of us about forty yards. There was something very tall moving down the hill and we all froze.

I was slightly ahead of the group and I asked Arla to come up front with me. I asked if she could see him.

She exclaimed, "OH MY GOSH, HE IS HUGE!"

He then made his way onto the moonlit path where we stood and stopped and stood there about forty feet away. The light of the moon reflecting off his lighter colored hair making him appear white.

Arla told me, "Keith, go up to him and talk to him."

I was not afraid, but the energy in the air was extremely strong. The hair on my neck and arms was standing up and the feeling was exactly like the charged air of an electrical storm. Words cannot adequately describe the feeling I had as he stood there. I walked up about twenty feet closer until I was within mere feet of him. I told him who I was and he simply gradually nodded his head ever so slightly.

Forest Friends of the Night

I was not afraid, but I was shaking with the feelings I was having. I stood there for a while and my head began to be flooded with thoughts. I could hear voices that were hard to understand and my mind swirled. I felt like I had information transferring into me. I could understand at that time that he KNEW who I was and he would visit me many more times. I felt a peace after about five minutes and that was it. He was still standing there but my time was over.

I stepped back and then I told Arla to go forward. She did for a couple of minutes but I was so taken aback I was simply watching and thinking about everything. When Arla came back, my wife Cathy wanted to step forward. As she was standing just in front of me, I noticed her left leg lift a little, about six inches out in front of her. She stayed but a very few minutes and returned. As she stepped back, he turned and walked away, down the trail then up the hill.

We turned and walked back down the trail to where we had parked. This time they followed us all the way to the road. Scott could hear them walking very well even as far as the road. I listened in the parabolic and we could hear them walk away after a few more minutes. As we stood there, I felt exhausted from the excitement and adrenalin rush. We gathered ourselves and then drove back to camp.

Forest Friends of the Night

We arrived at camp and I was so emotional and exhausted about what had happened, I never really said much to anyone at that time. It wasn't long, though, until DM, Jonathan and a few others came back from the home of our hosting couple where they were having their experiences.

DM was very excited and told me he had finally had his visual. He told of how the bigfoot person had looked around the tree at him and he got to see the big guy along with the eye glow that he described as being what we had witnessed a few months ago in the Spring. He was very excited here is his write up of that night, told in his own words as he experienced it:

DM: *"After a year of constant validation, glyphs, noises and signs... I got my first ever glimpse of one. I will remember that moment for the rest of my life. An individual showed himself to me at night at a range of twenty yards and I will never be the same. At first I saw a single dim orange glow in the dark... it went away... then I looked away and back again and the light had returned. After staring at it and asking if it was one of them I saw the large body move, along with the glowing eye behind the tree... I could only smile. It then stepped out again but with both eyes shining this time... I asked it to shine brighter and its eye ignited*

Forest Friends of the Night

bright red like LED flashlights and stepped off when I called someone over. I am still smiling ear to ear.

Later that night I headed by myself at around one am into a dark part of the woods where another member had had a life changing encounter. I felt I needed to head alone with no light source. Once I entered the area I could feel an energy in the air and then heard a massive individual walking very close to my left... there was no question as to what I was hearing and they were only doing it for me to hear... I was feeling quite nervous... I had to calm myself down then I spoke to it. I proceeded to walk deeper into the woods then heard a grunt... and another individual approached and followed me on the right. I felt at peace and spent an hour there listening to them around me. I'm excited for what is in store down the road. Pure heart and mind is the key... and the past year has led me to this mindset. I'm forever grateful for the people there that have entered into my life that I now treat as family."

There were many discussions while sitting around the fire this night. All of the activity that had been going on at night... the howls... the walking around the tents after dark... the many different sounds and things being moved around at night. They seemed to love hanging out around the cook tent and the food found there. Here are some of the actual write ups of some of the members that were there:

Forest Friends of the Night

Brenda: *"WOW, there was so much going on... Where do I start? The first night Robin and I got eye shine from at least three different bigfoot. This was behind the toilet house and playground. We also had what I call a bigfoot party going on with whoops and howls that just sounded joyful. On Friday night we were walking toward camp up the dirt road and, as we got near camp we had a very close, very clear grunt. Robin and I both heard that at the same time... Robin and I took many walks at dusk and deep night. We always got something. At one time we got something thrown at us and eye shine. We girls went to the shower house together and while we were hanging out there I saw one walk just inside the tree line that we had hiked through that day. This was in the same area Keith saw a black one. This one was black as well. Then Robin saw what she thinks was a brown one peek from behind a tree in the woods behind the Shower house.*

When we walked away from the shower house after dark one of the nights I saw a white light with a red trail streak through the pavilion. I looked around and there was no explaining it. Walking into camp after dark the night Raven was still out of his tent, I saw a large dark movement in the brush by Arla's vehicle. Our last night Robin and I went for a trek with Jason. We found a glyph on the trail and while walking I heard sounds behind me several times and I felt we were being followed.

Forest Friends of the Night

Once back in camp I was talking to Keith and saw a black bigfoot walk behind several trees in a row behind our camp. I could see its arm swing. Every night I could hear bigfoot walking by my tent and heading toward Arla's set up. The last night I had just gotten into bed and settled down when I heard heavy footsteps coming out of the woods toward my tent. I heard him step on the Hinson's ground tarp... He took three steps which put him about five feet from my tent. I laid there trying to breathe and slow my heart rate down. I prayed that he would not scare Zach. Then I heard Farrel wake up. I was praying that he would not get the tar scared out of him either. It was an adventure.

Oh I almost forgot it was one of the first couple nights I saw an upright shadow run through the woods right behind Darrin's trailer... it ran down hill away from camp."

Gail: Day three, Excitement... as I awaited the arrival of Jonathan, Arla, and Thom...and Wado. The feeling you have as you know family is about to arrive... later in the week, I walked in the dark with no flashlight and wearing flip flops, with Arla, Keith, and Scott. Behind our tents, I caught the movement and the sound as one of our big guys left the bush where they waited for us. The energy I felt pulsing through my body was strong and felt wonderful. What did I see? I saw outlines of shadows, but I felt them, and I felt the red haired female behind me and to the right... I could also hear her make a humming sound, and I heard that at my home also... It sounds a lot like a insect but very different. Scott confirmed hearing the sound with the head set and microphone. I can't believe I walked and followed them in the dark way out of my comfort zone, and did not trip and fall...

The night I followed Keith to his special spot in the moonlight was awesome. The area seemed to pulse with energy... What did I see? I thought I saw the outline of the big male, but was not sure... But what I did actually see was a small, white being... less than three feet tall and very skinny... To my eyes he seemed to glow... I had NO FEAR... I wanted to go down the hill to meet him, but stood my ground beside Scott... I felt I should be invited by him to go and I did not feel the invitation... Why did he seem small to me, or was I able to view something completely different? I could feel the guards flanking us on both sides, when we went in, and left the area... But I could not see them, wasn't important to see them, just knowing they were there was enough... I'm so thankful, for my time in the woods with everyone... I am forever changed, and now I have to sleep at home with the lights off."

Anita: "I really had the opportunity to re-connect not only with a group of amazing people, but with myself as well. I made lifelong friends and strengthened friendships that had already started. The area was remarkable with obvious activity all over the place. *The primal power that surged through there was absolutely amazing. Hearing them scream and howl through the night... being touched on the arm by one... tuning in and feeling at one not just with them but with all of the area are things I will take with me always."*

Farrell: *"Watching Zach as he connected with them by walking around and just talking was amazing. He blew his whistle and got a whoop each time. When he clapped his hands he got foot stomps. He said they didn't like the claps. He saw all colors of eye shine. Once, with Robin, they got teeth clicks as they got close to the edge of the woods. My biggest thrill was listening to the very heavy foot falls as they approached and walked around our tent. Brenda was next to us and heard them too. I was frozen and for a while I forgot to breathe. I felt the ground shake under his weight. Thrilling."*

Darrin: *Went to bed around twelve and I woke up around three am for no reason laid there around twenty minutes, got out and checked on Raven, no one up, moon was bright, little fog, my door of trailer was slapped or long door handle was raised and let drop against door frame, I took it as a good bye because it was the last night, and a "X" was beside my trailer next morning.*

The last one was written by Scott. Scott told me it was OK to use his full name but I would rather not because he is not a researcher, per se, to put his name out in public. But he also wanted me to make sure to let all know he is a Chief Magistrate Judge and he wanted that heard to help provide credence to his story. This story is of an event that touched him and forever changed his life. Here are a few things that happened to him along with his trip to my area:

Scott: *"I have just now gotten to the point where I would like to share my experience of last October. Keith had told the story, but I wanted to give my perspective. The details may not be spot on, but it is what I recall... Of those in the story, please feel free to add to it.*

Last October (2014) was my first trip searching for the sasquatch people. I was behind my tent just looking and listening to the woods when Keith walked up with a set of parabolic ears. He said when he walked up, that he felt there were bigfoot around. With the parabolic, I could hear movement deep in the woods.

Keith left me there alone, and I tried to communicate. I let them know I was respectfully there, who I was, why I was there, and let them know I was without a camera. By the time Keith came back it was dark and he brought three others, Arla, Cathy, and Gail. When Arla first arrived she said she sensed multiple bigfoot. She talked to them as a mother would talk to a child... Sweet, soothing, and constant.

We stood in one spot when they start whispering: "eye shine one o'clock, eleven o'clock etc." I saw nothing. Keith pulled me in front of him, and the forest came alive. I could see the eye shine. One set was low, as if they were lying down. Two sets looked as if they belonged to children, and the last set was about seven feet off the ground at a distance of maybe fifteen feet. It was dark and I could see nothing else, but others seemed to notice the blackness of shadows and subsequent movement.

At one time, Gail said there was a female at three o'clock. I saw nothing, but when I directed the parabolic, I could hear a consistent intermittent sound coming from her location. When I placed the parabolic in the direction of the two little ones, there was also a sound coming from them, but it was more of an energy sound if that makes any sense. Only in those two spots would I hear those sounds. I was amazed, and in awe.

We left as Keith took us to what is considered the area of his teacher, and of a particular clan of bigfoot people. As we approached, there was a small bridge. Keith stated that we would be greeted by two bigfoot people, one on each side and that they would escort us in.

As we were walking the path, I held the parabolic at each perpendicular side. Holy crap... but I could hear distinct footsteps crunching through the woods. When we stopped, I would hear an extra step or two. They followed us down the path two hundred to three hundred yards. When we stopped, I could see eyes shining on the left and on the right within ten to fifteen feet of us. I would say there were at least six of them, including the two following us in.

Arla then said, "There is a big one at the end of the path."

The others could also detect him, because he enveloped any light at the end of the path. I asked Keith how big, he said at least nine feet, and it was his teacher. Arla pushed further while we stayed. She stopped half way between us and him. She called Keith down where they stayed for five to ten minutes. The moment Arla started forward down the path, I directed the parabolic in the direction of the end of the path, and I heard the same energy sound I had earlier with the two children. After Keith and Arla returned, the sound stopped.

We walked back and I'll be damned if those two didn't follow us to the bridge. I heard heavy footsteps the entire time.

I was blown away and forever changed. Honestly, what I heard and saw had a drastic emotional and mental effect on me for weeks."

As our trip wound down and the end approached, there was a sad feeling on Sunday as people were leaving. There had been so much happen and the events that many experienced changed lives forever. We all felt a bond and closeness as sharing life changing events often does. It was the beginning, for many, of a great adventure. It was further validation for some others and for me. I am the student to all of this. I have learned so much but I know it is the tip of the iceberg. I will simply continue my journey and learn. I also want to try and share with the ones wanting to hear. I know I may never know all of it in my lifetime, but that is okay too. The main thing for me is the respect part of this I have learned... Respect for them, myself and others. What a great lesson that is for mankind!

Keith Bearden